A CREATIVE STEP-BY-STEP GUIDE TO

URBAN GARDENS

A CREATIVE STEP-BY-STEP GUIDE TO

URBAN
GARDENS

Author
Sue Phillips

Photographer
Neil Sutherland

WHITECAP
BOOKS

CLB 4139
This edition published in 1995 by Whitecap Books Ltd.,
351 Lynn Avenue, North Vancouver, B.C.,
Canada V7J 2C4
Printed in Singapore
ISBN 1-55110-281-1

Credits

Edited and designed: Ideas into Print
Photographs: Neil Sutherland
Photographic location: Country Gardens at Chichester
Typesetting: Ideas into Print and Ash Setting and Printing
Production Director: Gerald Hughes
Production: Ruth Arthur, Sally Connolly, Neil Randles

THE AUTHOR

Sue Phillips began gardening at the age of four, encouraged
by her grandfather, and had her first greenhouse at eleven,
where she grew a collection of cacti and propagated all
sorts of plants. After leaving school, she worked for a year
on a general nursery before studying horticulture at
Hadlow College of Agriculture & Horticulture, Kent for
three years. For the next five years, she was co-owner and
manager of a nursery in Cambridgeshire, before joining a
leading garden products company as Gardens Adviser.
This involved answering gardening queries, handling
complaints, writing articles and press releases, speaking at
gardening events and broadcasting for local radio. In 1984,
she turned freelance and since then she has contributed
regularly to various gardening and general interest
magazines and has appeared often on radio and TV
programs. She is the author of seven published books. She
lives in a very windy village on the south coast of England
near Chichester and has a very intensively cultivated
quarter-acre cottage garden on solid clay, plus a vegetable
garden next door, which she looks after with help from her
husband and hindrance from a Persian cat.

THE PHOTOGRAPHER

Neil Sutherland has more than 25 years experience in a
wide range of photographic fields, including still-life,
portraiture, reportage, natural history, cookery, landscape
and travel. His work has been published in countless books
and magazines throughout the world.

Half-title page: Dwarf hybrid tea rose 'Sweet Dreams'.
Title page: Planting up a miniature rockery in a trough.
Copyright page: A striking but small-scale water feature.

CONTENTS

GARDENING ON A SMALL SCALE

Gardens are getting smaller. Years ago a 'small' garden was generally considered to be less than half an acre (about a fifth of a hectare). Nowadays, that would be a pretty big garden by anyone's standards, and even 'pocket handkerchief-sized' often seems like an over-generous description. People with their first home, the newly single, and those who have moved back to a smaller house on retirement, can all be faced with the same problem. What can you possibly do with a tiny garden?

Actually, there is a great deal you can do - and without spending anywhere like as much time or money as 'luckier' landowners. You can create a garden as a cameo cut from a bigger garden - a patio garden, a water garden, an oriental garden - or you can set up a complete full-sized garden in miniature. You can fill a small garden with small plants and intricate detail or you can make it a low-maintenance one - ideal for people who want pleasant surroundings but have other things to do as well. You can treat a small garden like a sophisticated outdoor room by 'decorating' it with garden furniture and potted plants, or turn it into a secluded retreat for wildlife, even in the middle of the city. It can provide fresh fruit and vegetables for your table and be a nice place to sit out and relax in - both at the same time.

The purpose of this book is to provide the inspiration to get you started, with all the basic information to enable you to plant and grow suitable species in ways that will help make your small garden uniquely enjoyable.

Happy gardening.

Left: A beautifully laid out small garden. Right: Even topiary is possible!

What is a small garden?

A small garden is not the poor relation of a large garden - very much the reverse. In a small garden, it does not cost much to feed the lawn or lay mulch matting between shrubs to suppress weeds, because there is not much lawn or shrubbery. Instead, you can spend money where it counts - acquiring interesting plants, good garden furniture and features such as arches, patios and pergolas - all of which, incidentally, create vertical space on which you can grow more plants without increasing your workload.

Small gardens can be whatever you want them to be. They can be low-maintenance and leisurely; paving decorated with pots and a background of shrubs or climbers, with plenty of comfortable seating. They can be elegant and sophisticated town courtyard gardens, where a few carefully chosen tender plants revel in the sheltered environment with formal features. Minimalist oriental courtyard gardens are a growing trend, combining low labor with high fashion. At the opposite extreme, small gardens can be paradise for plant collectors; the ground jostling with precious alpines or cottage garden treasures, with barely room to pick your way through on narrow paths or stepping stones. Or they can be miniature versions of large gardens - enthusiasts have fun finding scaled down plants to fit their scheme. But do not imagine that only small plants are suitable for small gardens. Some people enjoy the lush jungle look and deliberately choose to grow anything with huge leaves, spiky shapes and extravagant flowers, and over-plant the area to create an abundant effect.

Right: One of the secrets of the small garden that stays interesting is not to be able to see it all at once; add curving paths and corners so that you have to walk round to see everything.

Below: A complete miniature garden created from small alpines and dwarf conifers in a shallow container. Such arrangements need meticulous care and regular watering so that they look their best at all times.

Above right: *Add plenty of fine details, such as containers and small ornaments, changes of surface texture and contrasting plant shapes. Steps bring in a change of level even if they do not lead anywhere.*

Right: *Small gardens do not have to be colorful - a garden based on foliage can look cool and restful in the middle of a city. The shaped lawn makes a focal point for the very detailed planting featured here.*

Maintaining a small lawn

Because a small lawn is walked on much more than a large one, it is essential to look after it or, rather like a carpet indoors, it will quickly begin to look shabby. Unlike carpets, lawns renew themselves - but only look good if they can do so faster than they wear out. This is where lawn care comes in. Routine chores, such as mowing and shearing round the edges of flower beds, need doing every week in summer, and perhaps every three weeks in winter until low temperatures finally stop the grass growing. Small lawns also need regular feeding; use a spring and summer formulation lawn feed every six to eight weeks from mid-spring until late summer. Some products now contain slow-release fertilizer, so a single dose in spring is enough. If weeds or moss are a problem, lawn feeds are available that include a treatment - one application in place of a normal feed in spring is enough. Alternatively, you can 'spot treat' small areas of moss or weeds, using liquid lawn treatments, often sold in self-squirt packs. Odd weeds, such as daisies, can be lifted out by hand with a daisy grubber. In the fall, an annual 'spring clean' is also a good idea. The aim of this is to alleviate problems caused by soil compaction and the natural cycle of debris production that occurs in a lawn, both of which prevent the grass growing properly. After mowing, rake the grass thoroughly to remove dead, creeping grass stems, then spike it with a garden fork every 4in(10cm), going down 2-3in(5-7.5cm) to improve surface drainage. Mechanical gadgets are available to make the task easier. Then apply a fall lawn feed as directed by the manufacturer.

1 If the soil is compacted, spike it with a garden fork. Rock the fork back and forth to loosen the soil below the surface, too; repeat every 1-2in(2.5-5cm) across the bald patch.

2 Remove a little of the surface soil, particularly any containing dead roots and weeds, so that when it is flattened again, the patch will be level with the surrounding lawn.

Right: *Where a lawn butts up to irregular stone paving, it is fun to exaggerate the uneven edge, but bear in mind that it takes longer to edge round the lawn after mowing.*

3 Level the soil roughly with a trowel, then sprinkle a little peat over the surface to improve the soil and improve its moisture-holding ability, ready for sowing seed.

Below: A long narrow garden divided into two 'rooms' gives the illusion of making the garden shorter but wider. Here the lawns are framed by shrubs and flowers to create a mini vista.

4 Sprinkle grass seed thinly over the area. As a guide, allow one ounce of seed per square yard, or roughly two seeds every centimeter. Sow it as evenly as possible.

5 Barely cover the seed with a little more peat or seed potting mix. Firm it down gently with your hand - the area should now lie flush with the surrounding lawn.

6 Water well in, and keep the area watered in dry spells. If birds are a problem or drying out seems likely, cover the area with crop protection fleece until the seed comes up.

Small mixed borders

To look effective, small gardens need to provide color and interest all the year round, and the best way of doing that is to have as many different kinds of plants as possible, including plenty of evergreens. By using compact kinds, you will be able to fit in more plants, which makes it easier to have something of interest at all times. A traditional mixed border, which uses shrubs, summer flowers and spring bulbs, is one way of ensuring plenty of variety. These are best arranged so that the taller, and especially evergreen, shrubs form the background planting and the outline shape of the planting scheme remains visible even in winter. Bulbs and low, ground-covering plants grown under deciduous shrubs provide interest when the shrubs are not flowering, and create a two-tiered planting effect. Any seasonal gaps can be filled with annuals.

Right: A mixed border of compact perennials looks most impressive backed by a framework of rustic poles or fencing used to support taller flowers or climbers, such as roses.

Traditional borders run round the sides of the garden, but nowadays island beds are popular. Being surrounded by lawn, they are easier to look after as you can reach them from all sides. The usual way of planting beds is to put the tallest subjects at the back or middle and shortest round the edge, but this can look rather predictable and it does no harm to put an occasional taller plant towards the front to interrupt the view. And instead of growing plants of roughly the same size, it is a good idea to have one or two 'special' plants as focal points. A small tree (see page 90-91), a striking architectural shrub, such as yucca, or a climber growing over an old tree stump or up a pole all make good central features.

Left: Annuals are a good way of providing long-lasting color in a small space throughout the summer months. The secret of keeping them flowering is to remove dead flowerheads regularly every few days.

Right: Containers are a useful way of filling seasonal gaps in the border with instant color. Their plain sides contrast well with the surrounding plants. Here, white tulips nestle alongside foxgloves.

Right: *A garden based on evergreens keeps its well-furnished look all year round. The foliage makes a good background for patches of seasonal color, and the winding path suggests the garden is longer than it actually is.*

Traditional borders for small gardens

Traditional herbaceous borders are basically summer displays, or at best spring and summer ones. Because they are made up solely of herbaceous plants, they look totally bare in the fall and winter. In a traditionally large garden this would not matter, as there is room for winter attractions elsewhere. However in a small garden, a herbaceous bed is a luxury, best kept small, and situated somewhere that needs a brilliant splash of summer color. Alternatively, you can adapt the idea to give it more year-round appeal by incorporating evergreens. Use a striking, medium-sized evergreen, such as *Photinia* 'Pallete' to give an island bed an evergreen center, plant herbaceous flowers around it and add an evergreen edging of dwarf box or clipped rosemary. Or create a mixed border using compact evergreen shrubs with specially good foliage, such as *Hebe* 'James Stirling', euonymus or phormium, with herbaceous flowers for a more informal effect. Bear in mind that most traditional herbaceous flowers grow too tall for a small border and would quickly overwhelm compact evergreen shrubs. They also need a great deal of staking to keep them upright. The solution is to grow compact varieties; nowadays, there are compact forms of most of the popular traditional herbaceous flowers. You will find them in garden centers and through specialist mail order catalogs. As a bonus, they often flower longer or more spectacularly than the full-sized version. Compact herbaceous flowers do not need to be supported, except in windy areas, when all you need to do is stand a 'cage' over the plant through which it can grow up.

Naturally compact herbaceous plants

Alchemilla mollis
Astilbe, Astrantia
Bergenia
Brunnera macrophylla
Dianthus
Erysimum
Hosta
Heuchera
Ophiopogon planiscapus
'Nigrescens'
Sedum spectabile

Left: *A gravel walk between borders gives a traditional feel to this small garden. The formal edging of clipped box and a background of trees and shrubs add a long-lasting framework of foliage to seasonal flowers.*

Above: *Bamboos and a fig tree flopping over an arch provide the background foliage for this cottage-style garden packed with geraniums, nepeta and poppies. A tall background helps to blank out surrounding houses.*

Above: *Filling a small garden with flowers is a good way to make the best use of space. Here, a grassy path leads to some garden ornaments that together with a background of conifers provide year-round interest.*

Right: *Narrow paths winding between beds of plants make a good background for flowers, and deceive the eye into thinking that the garden continues out of sight round the bend - a useful device in a small garden.*

All-year-round beds

The logical answer to the problem of providing all-year-round color and interest in a small garden is to use only evergreen plants, but you soon get bored with a garden made entirely of dwarf conifers, compact evergreens and ground-covering plants, as the view stays virtually the same all year round. Yet by adding a few seasonal touches - spring bulbs, grasses, and perhaps a few favorite flowers, you can soften the effect and still have a garden that needs little maintenance. Spend time designing the scheme, using pictures cut out from catalogs to judge the effect. Use the largest conifers and evergreens plus a few small trees as the backbone of the scheme, and a carpet of low spreading plants such as winter-flowering heathers, hebe, prostrate junipers or ivies to cover the ground in between. Use non-invasive ornamental grasses, bulbs, and other flowers as occasional highlights wherever a colorful contrast seems called for. The end result should look pleasantly undulating with a good range of plant shapes and foliage textures, and colorful seasonal highlights. A similar scheme can be created on acid heathland soils, using ericaceous plants. Dwarf conifers and birches will grow happily here, as will compact shrubs, such as dwarf rhododendron, pernettya, kalmia, pieris, fabiana and skimmia. Spread a mulch of bark chippings between the plants to retain moisture and suppress weeds.

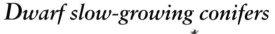

Above: Gaultheria procumbens *(checkerberry) is a good choice for ground cover on acid soils. Summer-flowering heathers and low vaccinium species (cranberries) are also possible.*

Dwarf slow-growing conifers

Juniperus communis 'Compressa'

Cryptomeria vilmoriniana

Picea mariana 'Nana'

Chamaecyparis lawsoniana 'Golden Pillar'

Chamaecyparis pisifera 'Compacta Variegata'

Taller growing conifers

Juniperus scopulorum
'*Skyrocket*'

Chamaecyparis lawsoniana
'*Allumii Gold*'

Chamaecyparis lawsoniana
'*Chilworth Silver*'

Above: *By using a mixture of compact and taller growing conifers, you can create an undulating landscape that needs no clipping or pruning. Add grasses, bulbs, heathers and a few containers of annual flowers for seasonal highlights. These will not add much to your gardening workload.*

Chamaecyparis
lawsoniana
'*Ellwood's Pillar*'

Do you really need a lawn?

Lawns may be traditional, but they are by no means essential. A small lawn needs a great deal of maintenance to keep it looking good and this means expense, too - fertilizers, tools, equipment - all of which need to be stored somewhere. What is more, if the garden is permanently shady or on poor soil, a lawn may never really thrive. It is hardly surprising, therefore, that many small garden owners decide to do away with their lawns. There are several alternatives. In a very tiny space, paving is not unduly expensive, and once down is virtually maintenance-free. You could create a very attractive low-maintenance courtyard garden, with climbers round the walls, fountains, statuary, seats, and choice plants in raised beds. In a sheltered, shady spot, a woodland garden is highly practical, using slitted black plastic or landscape fabric to cover the soil, hidden under a 2in(5cm) layer of bark chippings. Timber 'stepping stones' can make a path through shade-tolerant plants put in through crosses cut in the fabric. In a sunny situation, you could create a gravel garden using the same basic technique to smother out weeds, but with gravel, stone slabs and heat-tolerant plants. Alternatively, if the area will not receive much wear, you could make a herbal or flower lawn. A sunny site and well-drained soil are essential. Suitable plants include chamomile (the non-flowering form 'Treneague' is used for lawns), creeping thymes or spreading rock plants, which can all be planted as a carpet, with gravel paths or 'stepping stones' where you need to walk.

Right: Where open spaces are not needed for children and pets to exercise, a 'walk-thru' garden of shrubs and brick or paved paths looks interesting and makes good use of the limited space.

Left: Paving makes a good subsitute for lawn in tiny gardens. Grass would not withstand the inevitable heavy use without quickly looking worn.

Right: Gravel makes an informal back-drop for plants and containers, as well as providing cheap but low-maintenance ground cover. Rake it occasionally to keep it looking fresh.

Thymus x citriodorus 'Aureus'

Thymus azoricus

Above: A herb lawn, such as this chamomile feature, will not take much wear, so either provide paths around it or stepping stones across it.

Thymus lanuginosus

Chamaemelum 'Treneague'

Thymus serpyllum albus 'Minimus'

Planting through gravel

All too often, low-maintenance gardens look dull, as the easiest way of avoiding chores is to eliminate all the work-producing features - and along with them all the interest from the garden. But one way of having a garden that is quick and easy to look after, yet full of interest, is to create a gravel garden. Here, plants are grown in beds covered with a deep mulch of gravel, which suppresses weeds and helps retain moisture. However, unlike a conventional organic mulch that slowly rots, gravel lasts forever. To make the mulch totally effective against weeds - even persistent perennial ones - the answer is to put gravel over a layer of plastic (which needs to be perforated to allow the soil to 'breathe'), or over special heavy-duty woven plastic landscape fabric. The most suitable plants for growing through a permanent mulch are trees, shrubs, roses, conifers, perennial herbs and shrubby rock plants, as these all have a definite main stem around which you can tuck the plastic. Bulbs and herbaceous plants are not very suitable for growing where plastic is used under gravel, because the clumps spread under the surrounding plastic mulch, which smothers out the new growth around the edge. They also need lifting and dividing every few years. Nor are annuals practical, as they need replacing every season. If you want to incorporate these plants, the answer is to set aside special areas where the plastic is excluded, leaving only gravel. Many garden plants, especially rock plants and hardy annuals, will seed themselves very happily into a gravel-only mulch, and the result can look very natural and pretty. Simply pull up any that appear where you do not want them. However, expect weeds to appear too, so be prepared for a certain amount of work.

1 Prepare the ground in the usual way before planting, rake it level and spread perforated black plastic or heavy-duty landscape fabric over the surface as a permanent mulch.

2 Spread a 2in (5cm) deep layer of pea shingle or gravel over the plastic, so that it is completely covered. If necessary, secure the edges of the plastic sheet with bent wire pushed through it into the soil to hold it down as you work.

3 Having decided where individual plants are to go, scrape away the gravel from the planting position to expose the plastic beneath. Pile the gravel up nearby.

4 Use scissors or a sharp knife to cut a large cross in the plastic. This needs to be at least twice as wide as the diameter of the pot to allow easy access for planting.

5 *Turn back the corners of the plastic to uncover a square of soil. Hold back the plastic by piling gravel or stones onto the corners so that it does not get in the way as you work.*

6 *Scoop out soil to make a planting hole slightly larger than the size of the pot the plant is growing in. Place this carefully into a bucket, as weeds may grow in soil left above the plastic.*

7 *Knock the plant out of its pot without disturbing the roots. Lift it into the prepared planting hole, with its best side facing forwards.*

8 *Fill the space around the root-ball with some of the spare soil. Tuck the flaps of plastic back round the plant, covering the top of the rootball.*

9 *Replace the gravel over the plastic mulch. Hold back the stems so that you can be sure of pushing gravel right up close to the neck of the plant.*

Grouping plants in gravel

1 *When planting a group of plants in gravel, it is best to make a separate planting hole for each one to avoid creating large areas of open soil in which weeds could get a hold.*

2 *Since gravel reflects a great deal of heat in a sunny situation, choose plants that thrive in hot, dry conditions. For maximum effect, select plants with contrasting shapes, colors and textures. Allow prostrate plants to lead away from upright shapes.*

A gravel garden has a special ambience of its own that lends itself to certain styles of planting. Gravel naturally suggests a hot, dry Mediterranean-style garden, and indeed by reflecting heat back up, it can be the ideal way to 'warm up' a small courtyard or patio. To enhance this feeling, choose aromatic plants and strong architectural shapes - spiky plants, such as *Yucca* and *Cordyline*, Chusan palm, spires of *Verbascum bombyciferum*, ornamental sages, lavenders and rosemaries, plus pots of pelargoniums. A gravel garden can also look cottagey, combining meandering gravel paths with self-seeded hardy annuals, tumbling rock plants and cottage garden favorites growing among a tangle of roses and climbers. Formal herb gardens, too, often use gravel for their outlines, with a series of concentric gravel paths linked by radiating 'rays' from the center of a geometric pattern.

Gravel teams naturally with other hard materials, especially terracotta and stone, so make good use of 'props', such as bird baths, sundials, pots and urns for decoration. Break up large expanses of gravel path or a parking area by insetting occasional paving slabs as 'stepping stones'; circular or hexagonal slabs look especially striking. Distinct groups of plants, such as a trio of junipers - a spreader, an upright and a bushy variety would make an interesting focal point. Or go one step further and create a 'stone' garden, which relies on different textures for its interest. In this case, a larger area of gravel is punctuated by artistic chunks of rock, areas of cobbles or fine sand, and decorated sparingly with groups of trees and junipers. This scheme would be ideal in a modern setting between buildings, but it can also look great in a clearing in woodland and in other apparently unlikely situations. Be bold and experiment!

Below: *This unusual 'seaside' feature uses cobblestones set into pea shingle over soil. It is planted with* Echeveria glauca *and* Mesembryanthemum.

4 A group of plants can be a vague, informal shape, as if they had arrived naturally. Complete the scene by adding some architectural interest - containers, chunks of stone, large pebbles, a gnarled tree root, or perhaps a low birdbath.

3 Use low, sprawling plants around the edge of a group, with taller upright kinds to the center or back, to create an 'island' of plants in which each one shows up as an individual.

Red hot poker (Kniphofia)

Juniperus communis 'Compressa'

Hebe 'Sutherlandii'

Above: Sprawling rock plants provide welcome mats of color in a gravelled area; these are Linum arboreum *and* Erinus alpinus, *growing with homeria - an unusual, slightly tender, spring-flowering South African bulb.*

Below: Dwarf bulbs also appreciate the warmth and good drainage of a gravel garden. This is Sternbergia lutea, *which flowers in the fall.*

Golden marjoram

Helianthemum 'Ben Fhada'

Plants for all-year-round containers

Choisya ternata *'Sundance'*
Clematis
Cordyline australis
Dwarf rhododendron
Hebe franciscana *'Variegata'*
Miniature roses
Patio peaches
Phormium
Trachycarpus fortunei

Containers in a small garden

In a small garden, containers are useful for turning otherwise unproductive space - paving, paths, steps, etc. - into colorful features. Stylish containers also help to establish the character of the garden, and it is worth buying matching sets of attractive, good-quality containers made of frostproof terracotta or painted and glazed ceramics. Although initially expensive, these will last for many years and look much better than cheap plastic containers. A wide range of planting schemes is possible. Annual bedding plants are the traditional choice, and provide maximum color during the summer months. In the fall, you can put away the containers for the winter or replant them for a spring display. Alternatively, you can create a low-labor, all-year-round scheme using shrubby plants. Small trees could be trained flat and stood against patio walls where there is no soil bed. Since flowering shrubs tend to have short flowering seasons, it is best to create an all-year-round display using a mixture of flowering and foliage plants, including plenty of evergreens.

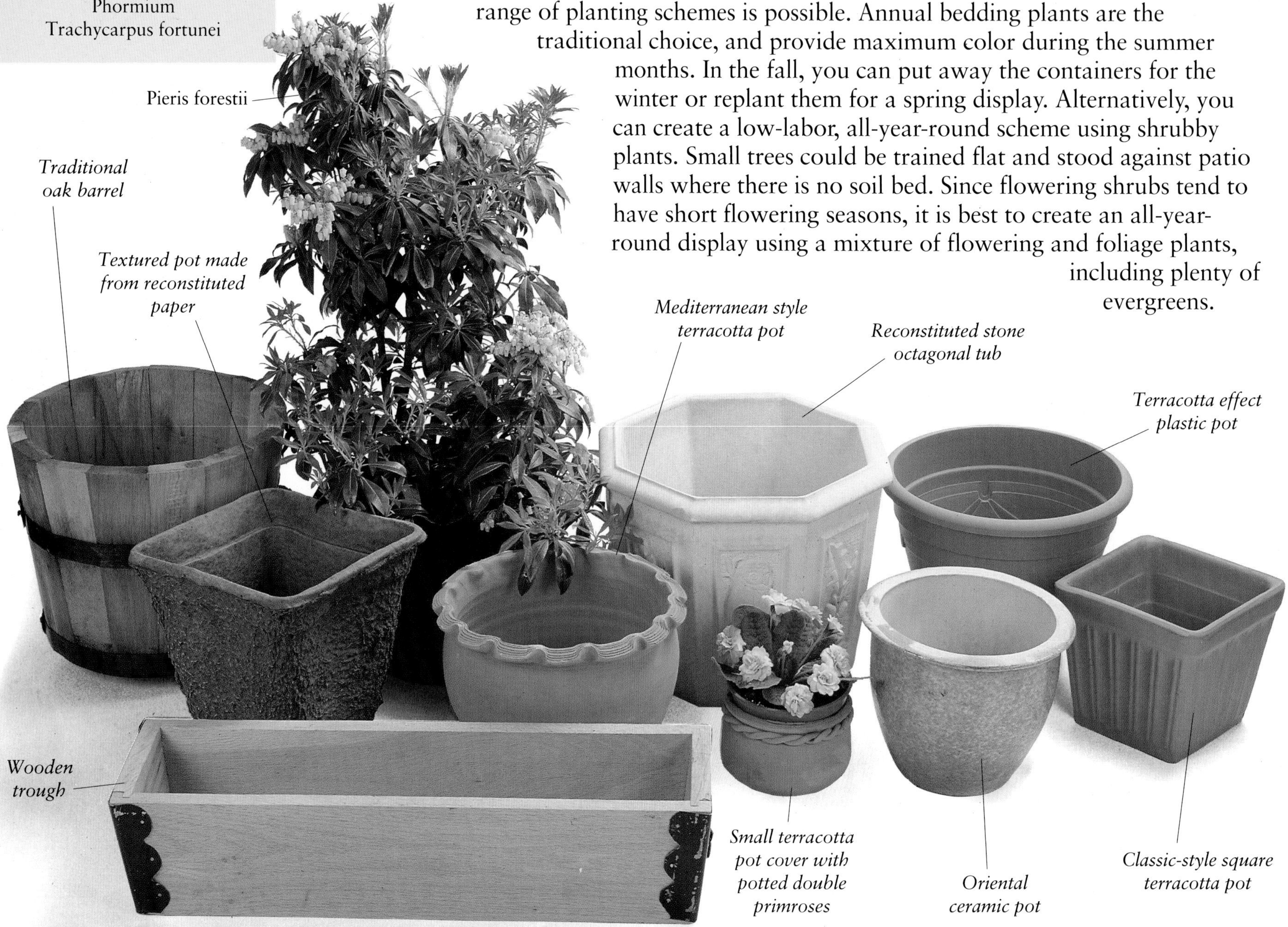

Pieris forestii
Traditional oak barrel
Textured pot made from reconstituted paper
Mediterranean style terracotta pot
Reconstituted stone octagonal tub
Terracotta effect plastic pot
Wooden trough
Small terracotta pot cover with potted double primroses
Oriental ceramic pot
Classic-style square terracotta pot

Below: *Terracotta pots of different designs planted with wallflowers, tulips and pansies make a fine spring display positioned on the edge of this brick patio. Remember to keep the pots well watered during dry spells.*

Right: *Instead of putting containers away for the winter, fill them with winter-flowering pansies, which will provide color during mild weather from late fall until midsummer. Keep them close to the house for shelter.*

Above: *A jumble of tender perennials - pelargoniums, argyranthemum and trailing lobelia - in terracotta pots give an informal, cottagey look when grouped together in a paved corner.*

A rockery in a trough

1 *Select a suitable container with several holes in the base. This one is actually made from styrofoam. Place 1in(2.5cm) of gravel in the bottom to improve the drainage.*

Few gardens today have room for a conventional rockery, but a miniature version in a container makes a most attractive feature on paving near a back door or seat. Team rockery-themed containers with gravel or cobbled paths, or tuck them into odd sunny corners around the garden. Stone sinks were once the traditional containers for alpines, but you can use virtually any sort of container, as long as it can withstand exposure to frost and has good drainage. Large terracotta pots, deep ceramic dishes and plastic troughs are all suitable. Check that there are plenty of holes in the base, and if not, drill more. Nurseries and garden centers offer a huge range of rockery plants, but vigorous spreading kinds will soon become a nuisance in a confined space, so restrict yourself to compact cushion- and bun-shaped plants. If you choose spreading plants such as aubretia, which make carpets of color, place them at the edge of the container so they can trail over the sides and make sure you can replace them easily with smaller plants when they outgrow their welcome. Since the majority of popular rock plants are spring-flowering, include plants with attractive, preferably evergreen, foliage to keep the display looking good all year round. You can also find ultra-dwarf trees such as *Betula nana*, to help create mini-landscapes.

2 *Place the largest rock in position before filling the container with potting mixture. This way it is easier to move around, and will look more natural partly buried.*

3 *Fill the container almost to the rim with soil-based potting mixture; this can be mixed with a small amount of fine grit to improve drainage even more.*

4 *Add a couple of smaller rocks to complement the larger chunk. Again, partly bury them in the potting mixture for a more natural effect and to prevent them becoming dislodged.*

Potted rockeries

Spring: *Trim back dead stems and sprinkle fresh gravel around plants. Feed with half-strength, general-purpose liquid feed when plants begin growing well and remove dead flowerheads.*
Summer: *Feed monthly as before and water the container well whenever the soil feels dry.*
Fall: *Remove any seedheads and sow seed straight away. Stop feeding; water only in dry spells.*
Winter: *Rock plants are at risk of rotting in winter, so ensure that containers are sheltered from excess rain and raised up on bricks, allowing surplus water to drain away quickly.*

5 Choose a selection of rock plants with different shapes, flower colors and leaf textures. Stand the pots roughly in position while you plan where to plant each one.

6 Knock each plant out of its pot, and scoop out a hole in the potting mix large enough to take the roots comfortably. Avoid breaking up the rootball of the plant.

7 Topdress with a layer of fine grit, which helps prevent the necks of the plants rotting. Raise the container up on bricks to ensure good drainage.

Primula auricula

Saxifraga 'Fleece'

Saxifraga cotyledon 'Southside Seedling'

Aubretia 'Blue Down'

Arabis fernandii-coburgii 'Variegata'

Oxalis adenophylla

Arenaria balearica

Saxifraga 'Silver Cushion'

Saxifraga 'Peter Pan'

Viola 'Molly Sanderson'

Saxifraga 'Cloth of Gold'

Sempervivum 'Commander Hay'

Silene 'Druett's Variegated'

Hanging baskets

You will find a huge range of hanging baskets in shops and garden centers, and most of them can be re-used for many years simply by replacing the potting mixture and plants at the end of each season. The traditional wire-framed kind must be lined before use. Moss or a modern substitute, such as coco fiber, is the traditional choice. These look good and allow a wire basket to be planted up through the sides as well as the top, but they do not hold water very well, so the basket drips and needs frequent watering. Alternatively, try rigid liners made of reconstituted paper and flexible fabric, or 'whalehide'. You can make your own liner by cutting black plastic or capillary matting (sold for greenhouse benches) to shape. These do not look so good initially, but you can cut holes in the sides to plant through so they will soon be hidden by flowers - and they improve water retention. Solid plastic baskets do not need lining and often incorporate their own water reservoir or drip tray, which saves them drying out so fast. If frequent watering is a problem, mix water-retaining gel crystals with the potting mix before planting up hanging baskets and wall planters, and line the inside of the container with absorbent fabric, such as capillary matting. Line porous containers with plastic. Automatic watering systems can be fitted up to take care of baskets on a regular basis.

Above: Pansies in a traditional wire-framed hanging basket form a complete ball of bloom that looks informal and cottagey.

Left: A hanging basket of Helichrysum petiolaris, fuchsias and Bidens 'Golden Goddess' here 'pulls together' all the elements around it - the door behind and the tiled floor below - by including flashes of color from each.

Right: Window boxes and hanging baskets make use of every available space, framing the cottage and transforming a tiny garden into a sea of color.

Traditional wire basket with a liner made of reconstituted paper. Note the 'push-out' panels for planting through the sides.

Plastic self-watering hanging basket

Hanging pot with built-in drip tray

Large traditional terracotta pot. Being porous, terracotta pots dry out quickly.

Plastic self-watering wall planter

Terracotta wall planter

Natural sphagnum moss. This water-retentive material is traditionally used to line baskets. There are many modern alternatives.

Coco-moss (natural coco fiber dyed green)

Coco fiber basket liner

Metal 'hayrack' wall planter (needs a liner)

A self-watering hanging basket

Hanging baskets suffer from one major drawback - they need an awful lot of watering. Size for size, they dry out much faster than containers at ground level, and in hot or breezy weather this can mean daily or twice daily watering. However, there are a few useful techniques that will help to keep them watered. One is to mix water-retaining gel crystals into the soil before planting the basket. (They can be added after planting, if you stir them carefully into the potting mix between the plants, but it is not possible once the container is full of roots). Another technique is to sink a plastic soft drinks bottle, with the end cut off, into the middle of the basket where it is hidden by plants. Use this like a funnel to channel water right into the heart of the basket where it cannot run out over the sides when you water. As an added refinement, leave the screw cap on the bottle and make a couple of pinholes in the neck so the water leaks out slowly and evenly during the day. (Add a few drops of liquid feed to the bottle, for beneficial 'little and often' feeding.) Alternatively, choose a self-watering hanging basket in the first place. These have a built-in water reservoir in the base, into which a 'wick' dangles from the planting space above. To prime the system, simply fill the reservoir and water the potting mix, and capillary action will do the rest. Depending on the size of the plants and growing conditions, the reservoir should last two to five days between fills.

1 Set out the assembled self-watering basket and a suitable selection of plants for summer color; here, we have chosen a cheerful display of Argyranthemum, Pelargonium, Verbena and Petunia.

2 Threequarters fill the basket with potting mixture. Lightweight peat or coir kinds are best in baskets. Avoid putting soil in the tube. Do not fill the water reservoir until planting has been completed.

3 Place the taller plants, such as the pelargoniums, between the attachment points for the chains, so that you get an uncluttered view when the basket is hanging up.

4 Use the smaller, trailing plants, such as petunia, to fill in the spaces around the front and sides of the basket. They will spill over and soften the straight edge.

5 Use taller flowers with a contrasting shape - these are verbena - to fill any gaps near the back of the display. They will add more color and a fuller shape.

Pelargonium

Argyranthemum

Verbena

Petunia

6 Hang the completed basket in a sunny but sheltered spot, making sure that the 'best' side faces front. Top up the reservoir every two to three days as necessary. Deadhead flowers regularly for continuous color.

7 When the basket is full, water the plants in the usual way until the soil is evenly moist. Then fill the reservoir in the base by trickling water down the pipe in the center.

35

Versatile hanging baskets

Left: Matching hanging baskets of tuberous begonia and trailing lobelia on either side of a doorway create a living frame of flowers. Make sure the baskets are within reach for watering.

Hanging baskets are great for making the most of wall space. They are usually hung from wall-mounted brackets next to a front or back door, or on a patio. However they can also be hung from pergola poles or on freestanding ornamental hanging basket frames, which are a good way of brightening up a patch of paving down the garden where there is no wall. Hanging baskets look particularly good teamed with other containers nearby, especially if they are planted with 'matching' flowers. Traditional basket favorites are trailing flowers, such as ivy-leaved pelargoniums, trailing lobelia, fuchsias and pendulous begonias, and compact annuals, such as busy lizzie and petunias. However, you can use all sorts of bedding plants; try nasturtiums, *Brachycome* (Swan River daisy) or morning glory. Baskets can contain all the same kind of flower, or a mixture of several different ones with foliage plants for contrast. You can use them for edibles, such as herbs and dwarf bush tomato plants, and in winter, provided the site is very sheltered, it may be possible to create seasonal displays using winter-flowering pansies, cultivated primroses and ivies. To do well, hanging baskets need a sheltered situation; in an exposed area avoid fragile plants or, better still, keep baskets under cover, say in a porch.

1 *Assemble a collection of 'tots' from a garden center. These are small plants in tiny pots, prepacked in a tray and ready for planting into an 'instant' basket at low cost.*

Healthy roots ensure that these small plants get off to a good start when they are planted out.

Being small, the plants need growing on for a few weeks before they start flowering.

Pelargonium

Multi-bloom pelargonium

Pelargonium

Petunia

Trailing verbena

2 *Plant up the 'tots' into a basket. This is a traditional, open-sided wire basket lined with natural coco fiber, an effective alternative to moss.*

3 *Put the completed basket in a sunny conservatory or greenhouse so that the plants grow up faster before they are put outside.*

Trailing ivy

Helichrysum petiolatum

Polygonum capitatum

Trailing fuchsia

Left: *These herbal hanging baskets containing curry plant (Helichrysum italicum), nasturtium and pineapple mint, look ornamental and are nicely scented when you brush past them.*

Right: *A single small container, simply planted, can look just as striking in the right situation as the more common 'mass-of-color' type of planting scheme. This terracotta hanging basket is planted with white pansies.*

37

Decorative wall planters

Making the best use of space is the secret of success when gardening on a small scale, and one of the prettiest ways of using odd bits of wall space is with decorative wall planters. These are like a cross between a hanging basket and a free-standing container, but they are divided in half down the middle and hang flat against a wall. They do not swing in the breeze like a hanging basket, and being flush to the wall offer the plants growing inside rather more warmth and shelter, so use them for your more delicate or heat-loving plants. They are the ideal way to display plants with a naturally floppy habit of growth, such as osteospermums, trailing fuchsias and pendulous begonias, which can spill forward attractively over the edges. Small trailing plants also look very effective. Take advantage of the favored situation to try some of the tougher indoor trailers, such as spider plant (Chlorophytum), wax plant (Hoya bella) and creeping fig (Ficus pumila) just for the summer. Wall planters can be used for longer trailing plants too, but the effect can be rather overwhelming unless you choose very large planters. Long trailing plants are probably best reserved for large hanging baskets. Normally, you put plants into potting mixture inside a wall planter, but there is no reason why you should not treat the planter like a decorative pot cover and stand a potted plant inside it. This way, it is easy to ring the changes and alter your display every week or two. This is a good idea in a very tiny garden, as it helps to keep it constantly new and interesting.

1 Wall planters are like half hanging baskets, so they do not need many plants to fill them. Part fill the planter with potting mixture and place the largest plant (here an osteospermum) in the middle.

2 This is a formal scheme, so tuck in a pair of identical plants (in this case Helichrysum microphylla) on either side to create a pleasing symmetrical arrangement.

3 Use a little more of the same type of potting mixture to fill the gaps between the rootballs towards the back of the display. Then water, and the planter is ready to hang up.

4 *Hang the planter on a warm*
sheltered wall that receives direct sun
for at least half the day. Although these
plants are fairly drought-tolerant,
water them daily
in hot weather.

Osteospermum

Above: *Pansies and violas prefer a*
cooler spot with shade from the hot
midday sun. Water them frequently,
as the container is so small.

Helichrysum
microphylla

Right: *A coleus*
hybrid forms the
centerpiece of this
planting scheme.
The French marigold
'Aurora' on either
side and the canary
creeper climbing
round the frame pick
out the yellow on
the coleus leaves.

Creating a Mediterranean-style patio in a small garden

The traditional patio originates from Mediterranean gardens, where summer sun and heat combined with seasonal water shortages made it impractical to grow a conventional garden of grass and flowers. Instead, the 'problems' were turned to advantage. Grapevines grew on a pergola overhead, and an outdoor living room was created in its shade, using paving and outdoor furniture decorated with terracotta pots of drought-proof plants, such as yucca, agave and pelargonium. On a sunny wall, bougainvillea was the classic climber. The basic pattern was taken up in other parts of the world and adapted, so that patios became a common feature on the sunny sides of all sorts of houses, ablaze with colorful climbers and bedding plants in hanging baskets and tubs all summer. However, this type of patio display needs frequent watering, feeding and deadheading to keep its looks. Now that a wider range of suitable plants and containers has become available, patios are becoming more individualized, and you can choose lower maintenance schemes. Busy people may prefer to grow shrubs permanently in containers to avoid the work of replacing annuals. Others find that a patio can be loosely interpreted to mean a courtyard-style garden that is open on one or more sides, with minimalist features - a few striking trees, shrubs or plant groupings growing in the ground, teamed with large - possibly empty - containers, imposing ornaments, and a range of interesting textures underfoot. It can be simply a paved area with low drought-tolerant aromatic plants, such as junipers and perennial herbs, growing in gaps where paving slabs are missed out. Or you can stand tender plants, such as lemon trees and succulents, outside for the summer to recreate the original Mediterranean flavor.

This Yucca gloriosa *will withstand frost and makes an ideal container plant. White, bell-shaped flowers appear in midsummer to fall.*

Left: *Exotic succulent plants, such as aeonium, aloe and yucca, join with the unusual* Pelargonium *'Freak of Nature' and scented-leaved pelargoniums in this heat-lovers patio.*

Left: *Concrete-rendered walls topped with pantiles create a Spanish-style background for a collection of drought-resistant plants grown in old stone sinks and terracotta pots.*

Below: *Frost-tender plants casually grouped by a seat for the summer: succulents* Echeveria, Dudleya *and* Agave americana *join with* Valotta purpurea *and* Helichrysum petiolaris.

Above: *Create a Mediterranean-style display by planting osteospermum, bay, Livingstone daisy, basil and cockscomb in a terracotta planter. Put the arrangement in a sunny spot.*

Creating a courtyard garden

A courtyard garden is the ideal solution for a small enclosed area that is to look good but requires minimum maintenance. With a hard surface, there is no mowing or weeding, leaving you free to concentrate on the decorative aspects of gardening, including stylish pots, plants and garden furniture. The design should look natural, with plants and features that lead you from one 'cameo' to the next, with a surprise round each corner. Thanks to the heat-retentive walls and flagged floor, a courtyard is usually quite well sheltered and in the mild microclimate it should be possible to grow slightly more tender plants than usual. Make the most of interesting textures by using piles of pebbles, natural stone and pea shingle as a change of surface and to outline specially splendid plants or your eating out area. And make the most of novel water features (see page 80) for sounds and sparkle, and scented flowers for extra interest. Formal gardens are coming back into fashion, and you can transform a tiny enclosed backyard into a very stylish outdoor room using classical features such as paving, gravel, urns, a few outstanding specimen trees, elegant statuary, fountains and seats. The formal garden relies heavily on architectural shapes of both plants and other features for its effect. Nothing is garish or cluttered; everything has its own space in which to show off its shape. Plants and pots complement each other perfectly; trees are outlined by classical arches or stand in alcoves. Climbers grow up columns. Topiary yews stand in gravel paths, and trimmed pyramids or standard box or bay trees are useful for pots on doorsteps.

The large-lobed leaves of Fatsia japonica *look particularly striking in a small arrangement.*

Left: *Create semi-formal 'alcoves' by arranging a small statue or other ornament against a background of foliage plants inside a frame of trellis or ironwork. This works well alongside a path or in front of a wall.*

Above: *Give a small enclosed garden a Mediterranenan 'feel', by using terracotta pots and roof tiles and filling up every available corner with brightly colored flowers, including plenty of bold daisy shapes.*

Above right: *Pineapple broom,* Cytisus battandieri, *makes a good shrub for a sheltered sunny wall. The large, cone-shaped yellow flowers are pineapple scented and appear in profusion during midsummer.*

Right: *Fill a small space with as much detail as you can, but put contrasting shapes, textures and colors next to each other so that each item stands out individually, otherwise all you see is an overcrowded mass.*

Potted topiary

Topiary has recently made a 'comeback' as a new gardening craze, but full-sized topiary trees need plenty of room and take years to train. In a small garden, topiary trees growing in pots are a much better alternative. You can buy them already shaped into pyramids, standard 'lollipop' shapes or spheres - at a price - though it is not difficult to train your own, given time and patience. The best plants for potted topiary are bay and box. After a bit of practice on the easier shapes, why not try out more complex designs of your own - miniature peacocks, teddy bears and sitting dogs or cats are all great favorites. To shape these, it is easiest to build a framework from rigid fencing wire to act as a permanent guide for trimming to. This also provides some internal support for the shape. It is also possible to buy ready-made topiary frames, which you can use to form 'proper' topiary, though you can cheat by growing climbers such as ivy over them for a faster effect. Although topiary has a formal air about it, trained trees in pots can be used in many different ways and will suit gardens of various styles. Stand a pair of pyramidal bays on either side of a doorway, or incorporate a row of standard trees in a formal garden, amongst grass, gravel or beds of annuals. Or use them to add height to a geometrical herb garden. Spheres are fun standing in a row along the edge of an informal flowerbed, or acting as a 'full stop' at the end of a border. They are at home even in informal or cottage-style gardens.

Left: All sorts of plants can be trained into unusual shapes; this fuchsia is being grown on a wire former by tying the new growth in place and stopping the side shoots to encourage it to thicken out.

Below: *Ivy makes a fast-growing topiary subject when trained over a suitably shaped framework. Tie the stems in place, fanning out over the frame, then 'stop' the shoots and clip to shape.*

Lengths of supple willow make up the framework beneath this neatly trained growth of ivy.

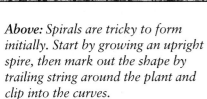

Above: *Spirals are tricky to form initially. Start by growing an upright spire, then mark out the shape by trailing string around the plant and clip into the curves.*

Left: *This topiary bird in a basket looks as if it may be in a nest, sitting on eggs - great fun for pride of place on a patio, or perhaps on shelves or staging in a 'vertical' garden.*

45

Shaping a box tree

Box is a very popular and easily managed traditional topiary subject. Use *Buxus sempervirens* and not the miniature cultivar 'Suffruticosa'. To shape existing box bushes growing in the garden or fair-sized bushy plants from garden centers, the best technique is to choose a plant that already suggests a simple shape, such as a bun or sphere, and simply exaggerate that by regular light clipping. The easiest way to create more complicated shapes is to start with a very small plant or, better still, rooted cuttings. Cuttings can be taken from established box plants at any time during the late spring and summer period. Snip 3in(7.5cm) pieces from the tips of the shoots and remove the lower leaves. Push them to two-thirds their length into pots or trays of seed potting mixture. Keep them moist and shady. When rooted - usually six to eight weeks later - pot each cutting into a 4in(10cm) pot and pinch out the growing tip to make it grow bushy. Nip out the tips of the subsequent side shoots so that the young plant is bushy from the base. Then start training.

1 *Start with a strong, rooted box cutting. Neatly nip off the growing tips of the shoots, using forefinger and thumbnail in a pincer movement. Repeat when the side shoots are 1in(2.5cm) long.*

2 *Use secateurs to nip back the tips of the next crop of sideshoots, so that each time the new growth reaches 2in(5cm) long it is shortened.*

3 *This regular pruning makes the plant bushier each time. At the same time as shortening the new growth, begin to roughly form the basic outline of the required shape.*

4 *Do not worry too much at this stage if the results are not very precise. The important thing is to have plenty of side shoots growing out in all directions.*

5 As the first pot becomes filled with roots, move the plant into a larger pot with fresh potting mix to keep it growing well. Continue clipping regularly with small shears.

6 By now, it should be possible to see a distinct shape emerging from the plant. Frequent clipping is very important while the shape is being formed, so that side shoots are regularly 'stopped' to keep the growth bushy and dense.

7 When it reaches the required size, clip back to the previous outline each time. By then, clipping three or four times a year should be enough.

8 Once large enough to clip, trim the tips of the young shoots back just enough to encourage branching, which gives a dense leafy shape, while allowing the shape to grow in size.

Above: Box balls in containers set out in a gap between clipped box hedges make a focal point in a formal setting.

9 It is possible to create a good box ball about 9in(23cm) across using this method in three years. Clip two or three times a year to retain the shape and size thereafter.

Trimming a bay tree

Bay trees are traditionally trained into various ornamental shapes: standard 'lollipops' and pyramids are popular. These are often grown in terracotta pots by a doorway or on a patio, or used to decorate a formal herb garden. Unlike box, bay has large leaves so it is not clipped with shears but pruned with secateurs, or even 'finger pruned' by nipping out the very tips of the shoots while they are tiny, to encourage branching. The large leaves also make bay unsuitable for training into very detailed shapes, such as spirals or peacocks, as it is not possible to achieve such a neat outline as with a small-leaved subject. However, it makes sense to train a bay tree, especially in a small garden, otherwise it quickly grows into a large untidy bush. A potted tree can be moved under cover during spells of cold, windy weather in winter, which might otherwise cause the ends of the branches to die back, or the evergreen foliage to be browned and spoiled.

1 To trim a pyramidal tree, such as this bay, make a tripod of canes and slip it over the tree so you can see at once which shoots are growing outside the required shape. Use a hoop of stiff wire to encircle the tree, outside the canes, as an adjustable pruning guide to ensure you end up with an even, conical shape.

2 Since bay leaves are quite big and their appearance would be spoiled if leaves were cut in half, it is best to prune them with secateurs instead of clipping them with shears.

4 The end result is a smartly trimmed bay tree. Do not expect to achieve a totally smooth outline, as you could with a small-leaved plant that has been clipped.

Above: Pinch out the tips of young shoots growing towards the edge of the desired shape.

Move the wire hoop to the area you are working on so you can constantly check what the ideal outline shape should be as you are pruning.

As a bonus, you can dry the bay prunings and use them fresh or dried in cookery.

3 Using the cane tripod as a guide, snip away any shoots that extend beyond the pyramidal outline, cutting just beyond a leaf so there are no bits of bare twig sticking out.

Here the pot is standing inside a terracotta pot cover. Do not plant into a rounded pot, as you cannot get the rootball out without breaking the pot.

The oriental approach

While few people wish to duplicate an authentic oriental garden in full, there are plenty of ideas worth 'borrowing' to help create a peaceful, low-maintenance garden in a small enclosed space. Oriental gardens are minimalist, making the most of relatively little material. They are not traditionally colorful, but rely mainly on the shapes of green plants set against raked gravel for their effect. Ornaments, such as gnarled trunks, rocks or pebbles and a stone lantern are traditional, as is a 'deer scarer' - a bamboo tube that is periodically hit by a striker, operated by water running through it. Running water is well known for its relaxing properties and the same effect can be achieved using water running from a terracotta jar into gravel, or gushing up through large stones. When planning an oriental-style garden, the space between objects is as much a part of the design as the objects themselves. Assemble your 'ingredients', including plants, and stand them out in several alternative settings to decide which works best. Fortunately, when so few ingredients are involved, it is not difficult to move things around if you want to rearrange them later on.

Right: *Assemble a collection of oriental-style shrubs and plants and some suitable 'props', such as a stone lantern, bamboo deer scarer device or, as here, plain smooth pebbles.*

Arundinaria (Pleioblastus) murieliae

Rhododendron yakushimanum *'Vintage Rose'*

Cryptomeria japonica *'Elegans'*

Azalea *'Gibraltar'*
(deciduous type)

Hosta fortunei
aureomarginata

Acer palmatum
'Dissectum'

Cryptomeria
japonica
'Vilmoriniana'

Picea mariana
'Nana'

Right: *A submersible pump installed in a container filled with pebbles is the secret of this feature. It is created in the same way as the 'potted pond' on page 76. Team it with a curtain of bamboos or a Japanese maple to complete the cameo.*

Below: *An oriental deer scarer. Water trickles into a hollow bamboo tube that tips over when full, so that the end strikes a larger hollow bamboo tube with a dull thudding sound. Though probably not all that effective at scaring deer, it is a traditional part of a Japanese garden, and the periodic sound is surprisingly restful.*

Creating a bonsai conifer

Good plants for an oriental-style garden include flowering cherry, almond, peach, ornamental quince *(Chaenomeles)*, rhododendron and azalea, bamboo and Japanese maple (*Acer palmatum* cultivars). Evergreens and conifers can be trimmed into approximations of bonsai shapes, even when they are growing in the ground. Another effective way of trimming them is to leave bare stems at the base of the plant and clip the foliage to resemble 'clouds' at the top. Good conifers for clipping include the blue-leaved *Chamaecyparis pisifera* 'Boulevard' and dwarf cultivars of C. *lawsoniana,* such as 'Green Globe'. Trees and shrubs that grow naturally into dramatic bonsai-like shapes without any need to prune or train them include the dwarf Mount Fuji cherry (*Prunus incisa* 'Kojo no Mai'), twiggy, upright *Prunus* 'Amanogawa', contorted hazel, and unusual weeping conifers, such as *Sequoiadendron giganteum* 'Pendulum'. Poorly shaped specimens of azalea and other oriental-look shrubs can be a cheap buy in garden centers and are easily pruned into lopsided 'bonsai' type shapes. A small collection of real bonsai trees in traditional tiny containers displayed on shelves or staging adds interest to this type of garden, but are best left to enthusiasts, as they need regular root pruning, wiring and daily watering. You can achieve a similar effect by growing traditional bonsai subjects (conifers, wisteria, oak, acers, pines, etc.) in much larger pots, in the same way as you would grow shrubs on a patio. These can be trimmed into freehand oriental shapes, just for fun.

1 Small and medium-sized conifers can easily be converted into potted oriental styles. It is a good way to use a less than perfect specimen.

2 Trim away the lower leaves to accentuate the trunk-like appearance of the lower stem, removing all dead leaves and shoots.

3 Prune out all brown leaves and bare shoots, so that everything left is green and healthy. Now you can start trimming.

4 Spread out the main branches to see the basic structure and decide how to shape it.

5 Thin out some of the growth from the base of the plant to start exposing the outline of the main branches growing out from the 'trunk'. The ultimate aim is to create a plant with a craggy, aged look.

6 Move to the top of the plant and thin the top to accentuate the shape of the main branches, leaving 'key' fronds of foliage towards the end of each large shoot.

7 Continue to thin out the plant. The aim is to produce an asymmetrical shape that looks as if it has been naturally sculpted by the wind. Shorten some shoots to leave stubs along the branches, for character.

Chamaecyparis pisifera 'Boulevard Variegated'

Rubbing the scales off the stems gives them a smoother finish.

8 Stop when you think you have done enough. The finished tree should have a good basic framework of exposed branches with a well-balanced spread of foliage towards the tips.

53

Hebe and ginkgo in oriental style

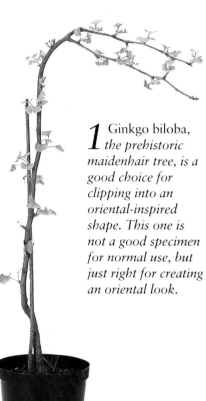

1 Ginkgo biloba, the prehistoric maidenhair tree, is a good choice for clipping into an oriental-inspired shape. This one is not a good specimen for normal use, but just right for creating an oriental look.

2 Bend the horizontal shoots over and tie them in place to accentuate the effect.

Some conifers and evergreens naturally grow into striking shapes that make them suitable for an 'oriental' display without much clipping and trimming. Alternatively, you could group a collection of choice, truly dwarf conifers and evergreens on a patio in matching weatherproof pots for a low-maintenance, all-year-round display. For compact, globular shapes, go for *Chamaecyparis* 'Gnome' and *Hebe* 'Green Globe'; for a compact craggy spire choose *Chamaecyparis obtusa* 'Tetragona Aurea', or for shaggy curls go for *Pinus mugo* 'Pumilio'. Since these are not being treated as true bonsai trees, choose pots of a suitable size for each plant and a soil-based potting mixture. After a year or two, the plants will need moving to a pot one size larger, preferably in spring. When a plant reaches the maximum desired size, repot it back into the same pot after trimming away about one quarter of the fine roots from the edge of the rootball.

Trimming a hebe

1 This Hebe 'Green Globe' has a naturally tight, compact shape that needs little trimming. Just tidy up the new growth.

2 Use single-handed clippers, sheep shears or even large scissors to give it a 'haircut'. Snip back the new growth to re-establish the solid outline. Start at the top of the plant.

3 Curve the top and progress to the sides, keeping carefully to the natural shape of the plant. Trim the plant once a year just after the main flush of growth to keep it neat.

3 Pull down the two shoots so that they lie roughly parallel, with one echoing the curve of the other. The shape should have 'set' within a year, and then you can remove the string.

4 Move the tree into a larger oriental-style pot. The top of the rootball should lie flush with the soil surface just below the rim of the new container.

5 Before completing potting, experiment by tipping the tree to see if you can create a better 'bonsai shape' by inclining the stem at an angle. An irregular shape often looks best.

4 New growth will soften the hard edges. Side shoots will appear from just below the cut ends, making a bushier shape.

Acer palmatum 'Atropurpureum'

Maidenhair tree (Ginkgo biloba)

Hebe 'Green Globe'

Handsome hostas

Hostas are fashionable and very decorative herbaceous plants, grown mainly for their handsome foliage. They are best known as plants for moist, shady conditions, but as long as the ground does not dry out severely in summer, hostas will thrive in sun. They are also good subjects for growing in pots and look particularly striking in glazed ceramic ones as part of an Oriental-style feature. Hostas are available in a tremendous range of cultivars, including some with thick, glaucous-blue leaves, cream or white variegated leaves, all-gold leaves, and also some with very small leaves. Although all hostas have flowers, many of them are not very striking. However, a few varieties have particularly good flowers - sprays of nodding bells in mauve or white - and some are faintly scented. As a group, hostas are very collectable; expect to pay more for the latest new cultivars than for older ones that have been available for several years. Prepare the ground well where they are to be planted, adding plenty of well-rotted organic matter to retain moisture. Mulch around the plants in spring and keep well watered in dry spells. Once planted, avoid disturbing hostas until the clumps are very large and really need dividing. Then dig them up, divide, and replant back into freshly prepared soil in spring. Some varieties will take a year or so to settle down and then start growing well. Hostas are particularly prone to slug damage, so either protect plants with slug pellets or mulch round them with coco-shell, which has the property of repelling slugs and snails. Growing in pots makes it easier to protect hostas in very slug-ridden gardens; simply apply a pest control 'glue' around the rim of the pot, or sit the container in a saucer containing 1in(2.5cm) of water.

1 Hostas are good subjects for pots, and by growing them in containers they are easier to protect from slug and snail damage. Partly fill the container with a soil-based potting mixture.

Left: *A single, specimen bonsai tree makes a good focal point in a patio; plunged into decorative gravel in a larger container it looks effective and watering is easier.*

Right: *An oriental-style garden relies on contrasting shapes and textures rather than color for its effect - this is deliberately done to create a restful ambience.*

2 Tip the plant out of its pot without breaking up the rootball, unless it is very potbound. Transfer it to an oriental-style ceramic pot, keeping it as central as possible.

3 Fill in around the edge of the rootball with more of the same potting mixture. Leave a gap of about 0.5in(1.25cm) between the soil and the rim of the pot to allow space for watering.

4 Water well in. Hostas need moist conditions and though usually recommended for shade, they will grow in sun if they are wet enough.

Protect the plants from rain if necessary. They should not become waterlogged.

Right: A properly housed collection of bonsai trees; the lath sides and roof create cool shade and provide just enough shelter, yet allow free air circulation around the plants.

Climbing plants

In a small garden, you must make use of all the available space, not only in your plot but also above it, by gardening in three dimensions. Walls, fences and screens offer plenty of scope for growing things upwards. Ivies and climbing hydrangea use suckers or aerial roots to hold on to a bare wall, but make sure the wall is completely sound. Vines, passionflower and clematis use tendrils or kinks in leaf stems to grip onto a trellis or netting; tie these in at first until the plants can hold themselves up. Climbing roses, wall shrubs and fan-trained fruit trees do not grip at all and new stems need tying to trellis or wires as they grow. If you have a large area of wall, you might choose a single, spectacular large climber instead of several smaller ones. Most perennial woody climbers are perfectly suitable for growing on walls and screens made of ornamental blocks; choose plants that do not need pruning if they are going to grow up out of comfortable reach. If you have a wooden fence, be aware of the need for maintenance, and choose climbers that either die down to ground level or need hard annual pruning. You could also grow climbers trained to trellis that can be lifted down when you need to work on the fence behind it.

Above: Tropaeolum speciosum *does best in a cool, humid climate, growing up through shrubs or on a wall facing away from the sun. Hard to establish, but spectacular where successful.*

Left: An unusual, striking combination: wall-trained pyracantha and climbing nasturtiums share the same support wires, but grow from opposite ends to avoid smothering each other.

Right: Mina lobata *(quamoclit) needs a very warm sunny wall to thrive and is best treated as an annual. The unusual flowers change through several different colors as they open.*

Below: Even in a small garden, a large climber can be just right. It is ideal if you have a large wall area and want an 'all-over' look. This is Actinidia kolomikta.

Below: Canary creeper (Tropaeolum peregrinum) *is a fast-growing annual climber useful for growing over rustic poles to provide height in a border.*

Left: Passionflower has striking but shortlived flowers. Give it a warm sunny spot and prune the previous year's growth back to within a few buds of the old stems in early spring.

Vertical gardening

Planted pillars, posts and pergolas are another good way of adding an extra dimension of space to a small garden. Brick pillars and wooden posts can be 'planted' towards the back of beds or built as free-standing features, or you can utilize existing pillars supporting an overhanging roof (of a car port, for instance). Clad them securely with wire or plastic netting to support the plants - this will soon disappear under the foliage. Use pillars and posts to grow self-supporting climbers, such as clematis and passionflower, and annual climbers, including sweet peas, morning glory or *Eccremocarpus* (Chilean glory vine). Avoid very large climbers that soon outgrow the space and dangle untidily from the top. Avoid roses too, as they only flower at the tips of the stems so that all the flowers are at the top of the pole; roses are better trained out horizontally over a wall. Pergolas, which incorporate a horizontal element, are traditionally planted with grape vines, but they are also a good place to grow scented flowers, such as honeysuckle.

Above: Turn the space under a fire escape into a beautiful patio, and disguise the stark metal of the steps with colorful hanging baskets.

Yet another way of adding vertical space to a small garden is by using several tiers to create different levels in an otherwise flat area. You can achieve the 'layered' look by growing plants in pots on shelves, staging and steps, and in raised beds. Shelves, elevated containers and raised beds are all good ways of growing plants that need special attention - and they are a striking way to display a much-loved collection. In a basement apartment, try growing shade-loving ivies on shelves, or if you have a sunny spot, alpines in raised beds. Cacti and succulents can occupy a strategic spot on a courtyard or patio in summer, and bonsai collections look striking on shelving or tiered staging in a sheltered spot.

Left: An arch adds height to a small garden and provides growing space for climbers. The rose used here is 'Excelsa'. Plant it on the sunny side of the arch.

Left: Use clematis, such as this 'Ville de Lyon', to cover trellis and provide slight shade, shelter and privacy to an enclosed area outside the house. Prune previous year's top growth in spring.

Make sure you can reach the plants at the top of the staging when they need watering. If necessary, use a long handle on the end of a hosepipe.

Left: A fruit tunnel is normally a feature seen in big gardens, but by using only two or three sections, you can create a large arch - and yet still pick a lot of apples from the space.

Above: Bank a collection of seasonal flowers in pots up on staging against a dark background to make a striking display. You can change the plants and pots as often as you like.

Planting a clematis

Clematis are versatile climbers for small gardens; they grow over arches, on trellis or netting on a fence or wall, through trees, up pergola poles and even in pots on a patio. The popular hybrids flower freely for much of the summer without growing too large. They fall into two groups; those that need pruning and those that do not. Cut 'do-prune' cultivars almost to ground level early each spring; these are the best sort to grow against fences where you may need access for repairs, or in pots, as it is easier to repot a climber when it has been cut back hard. 'No-prune' cultivars are the ones to grow through trees or where access is difficult. If you grow several different climbers together, say on an arch, choose those that need similar pruning since it is very difficult to separate them. (Plant climbing roses with 'no-prune' clematis). Tie the care label with the pruning instructions to the base of each plant. Grow clematis in moist, fertile, neutral to slightly alkaline soil, in a situation where their roots are in shade but their tops can grow up into sunlight. Most varieties need direct sunlight for at least half the day or flowering can be impaired. Clematis are heavy feeders, so give them a liquid tomato feed in spring, then a general feed every two weeks until midsummer. If you grow them in pots, choose the largest pot available and a rich soil-based potting mix. Keep well watered and apply a general-purpose liquid plant feed regularly throughout the growing season.

Below: 'Nelly Moser' - a large hybrid clematis that flowers in early and late summer. Do not prune or one flush of flowers will be lost.

1 First improve the soil with plenty of well-rotted organic matter. Dig a hole 4in(10cm) deeper than the plant pot, and at least 12in(30cm) away from the wall.

2 Sprinkle a small handful of general fertilizer into the hole and mix this well into the soil. Plant roots can be scorched if they come into direct contact with fertilizer granules.

3 Tip the plant carefully out of the pot without breaking the rootball. If roots are coiled thickly around the base, gently tease the largest ones out from the mass. Then lift into the hole.

4 Plant the clematis considerably deeper than when it was in its pot. In the event of clematis wilt, new shoots grow from underground stems.

5 After filling the planting hole, water the clematis in thoroughly. Give it a sufficiently good soaking so that the water penetrates right to the bottom of the rootball.

6 Tip the plant back against the trellis. Fix the cane to the trellis, then spread out the stems at the top of the plant and tie them in separately.

The stems will climb naturally up onto the latticework. They support themselves using 'kinks' in their leaf stems, so no more tying in should be needed.

7 Spread a thick layer of peat or similar well-rotted organic matter in a circle at least 18in(45cm) wide all round the plant. This helps to retain moisture around the roots and also keeps them cool.

8 The gap between a climbing plant and the base of the wall is essential. Close to a wall the soil is very dry and usually contains rubble forming the wall's foundations. Further away, conditions are better.

Coping with deep shade

Deep shade is often a problem under large trees, or in a garden surrounded by tall buildings. In both cases excess shade is usually combined with other problems. One of these is dry soil, caused by rainwater being deflected away from the soil, and what moisture there is being absorbed either by the trees or walls. In such situations the soil is also likely to be poor, due to the removal of topsoil during building operations, buried rubble, or tree roots close to the surface. Few plants will be happy unless the 'habitat' is improved. The canopy of branches can be reduced by tree surgery to let in more light, but be sure to obtain the permission of the owners of any trees that are not in your own garden. You should also check to see whether any trees are the subject of a preservation order, as you may need official permission to cut them back. With walls or fences, it may be possible to paint them white to improve light reflection into the garden. Soil is best improved by adding plenty of well-rotted organic matter. If tree roots are close to the surface, apply a thick mulch and top it up annually, as it will not be possible to dig it in. On the heavy clay found in many cities, add gritty sand as well (one bucket per square yard/square meter) as a natural clod cure. Then choose shade-tolerant plants. If you can keep the soil moist, then violets, hosta, ivies, Solomon's seal, hardy ferns and hydrangeas will grow well, and if the soil is slightly acid, you can add Japanese maples, camellias and dwarf rhododendrons. For summer flowers, bear in mind that *Impatiens* (busy lizzie) thrives in shade provided it has started to flower when it is planted.

These spring flowers give way to blue-black fruits.

Left: *In late spring, the arching stems* of Berberis stenophylla *are alive with golden-orange flowers. It makes quite a large shrub unless pruned.*

Below: *Epimediums are good ground-covering plants for shade.* Campanula latiloba, *a herbaceous flower seen here with it, grows in sun or shade.*

Right: Brunnera macrophylla *has large leaves (variegated varieties are specially good) and tall sprays of forget-me-not like flowers in spring and early summer. It spreads slowly in shade.*

Above: Hardy ferns and bergenia make an attractive plant association for shade; this is an unusual fern called Thelypteris phegopteris, *but a wide range is generally available.*

Vinca major 'Variegata', an excellent ground cover plant for shady situations.

Hedera helix 'Chrysophylla'

Euonymus fortunei 'Emerald 'n' Gold'

Aucuba japonica 'Variegata', a sturdy evergreen shrub with attractive yellow-spotted leaves. Ideal for shade beneath trees.

Hot and dry areas

Hot, dry, sunny spots may look ideal from our point of view, but they can be less than perfect for plants. One way of making the most of such a location is to use it for a patio. Alternatively, choose plants that enjoy these conditions, many of which are difficult to grow anywhere else. Only a limited range of plants thrive in poor, dry, unimproved soil - go for the winter-flowering iris *(Iris unguicularis)*, nerines, sun-loving euphorbias such as *Euphorbia cyparissias*, aromatic herbs such as rosemaries and sages, thrift, silver-leaved plants, such as artemisia, and fleshy sedums and sempervivums. But by incorporating plenty of well-rotted organic matter to help the soil hold moisture, you can add many more plants, including some that are quite exotic-looking. In a border try bottlebrush *(Callistemon citrinus)*, myrtle, Russian sage *(Perovskia atriplicifolia)*, the indigo bush *(Indigofera heterantha)* or the heathlike fabiana (which needs acid soil). There is a good choice of interesting and unusual climbers, too; try the pink, cream and green variegated *Ampelopsis brevipedunculata* 'Elegans' (a modest grower that is usually cut down to ground level by frost each winter) or *Trachelospermum asiaticum*, which has scented cream flowers in summer. Or, to create a shady area on the sunny side of the house, why not grow grape vines up pergola poles. Whatever you grow, one tip applies to all drought-tolerant plants: they are not drought-tolerant when first planted, so keep them well watered until they are properly established.

Above: Cistus lusitanicus 'Decurrens' is a low, compact evergreen shrub with large poppylike flowers in early and midsummer. It loves hot dry sites and roots easily from cuttings.

Myrtus apiculata 'Glen Gleam'

Artemisia 'Powys Castle'

Compact, drought-tolerant sunlovers

Agapanthus, Allium *(ornamental onion)*, Alstroemeria, Alyssum saxatile, Ballota, Cistus, Convolvulus cneorum, Dianthus *(Pinks)*, Euphorbia, *Geranium species (hardy cranesbills)*, Hebe, *Lavender*, Osteospermum, Nepeta, Santolina, Senecio *'Sunshine'*

Hebe *'Sutherlandii'*

Stachys lanata

Juniperus communis 'Green Carpet'

Helichrysum italicum *(curry plant)*

Sedum acre *(biting stonecrop)*

Left: *For a warm trellis or pergola in a mild location, the evergreen self-twining climber* Trachelospermum asiaticum *is hard to beat. The creamy midsummer flowers are fragrant.*

Right: *For a rock garden, scree or the front of a dry border, the diminutive* Geranium cinereum *'Ballerina' is a real charmer. It flowers continuously from early summer almost until fall.*

Rosmarinus
'Miss Jessup's Upright'

Hypericum x moserianum
'Tricolor'

Phlomis
fruticosa
(Jerusalem sage)

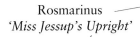

Santolina
chamaecyparissus
'Nana'

Melissa officinalis
'Aurea'

Hebe
'James Stirling'

Artemisia absinthium
(wormwood)

Compact shrubs

Like trees, shrubs vary in size and vigor. With the aim of creating an 'instant garden', most people, make the mistake of filling up borders with vigorous shrubs that quickly become overgrown, then try to salvage the situation by heavy pruning. This just makes vigorous shrubs grow even more vigorously, and often prevents them from flowering - a complete waste of space. It *is* possible to grow large and vigorous shrubs in a small garden if you do not mind 'thinning' the border by removing alternate shrubs after a few years to allow the remaining ones to develop properly. But it is much better to choose slow-growing or compact kinds in the first place, as this way you can fit in a larger range of plants and the result will automatically be more interesting to look at. Compact shrubs can be planted closer together than large-growing kinds as they stay neat. Combine them with low, creeping shrubs and a thick mulch for an attractive, low-maintenance border. Alternatively, space them a little wider apart and use them as the basis of a mixed border (see pages 16-17).

In selecting compact shrubs for a small garden, choose a mixture of plants that provide colorful flowers, evergreen foliage, fruit and, perhaps, fall color or architectural shape, so that they earn their keep all year round. Shrubs that are naturally compact rarely need pruning. All you need to do is to go round in spring with a pair of secateurs removing any dead or diseased shoots, plus any where the tips have died back as a result of frost damage. Cut these cleanly back to their junction with a healthy branch. Feed compact shrubs in spring and summer with a general-purpose plant food to maintain good growth. (Use rose food if you are feeding roses anyway).

Prunus triloba 'Multiplex' is a flowering cherry bush with double pink flowers in spring.

Hebe franciscana 'Variegata' grows to 18x18in(45x45cm). This variegated evergreen has purple flowers in summer.

Convolvulus cneorum *has silver foliage, and pink, funnel-shaped flowers in summer.*

Spiraea x bumalda *'Gold Flame' is a deciduous shrub that grows to 30x30in(75x75cm). Prune it hard to maintain the gold coloring.*

Left: Convolvulus cneorum *makes an attractive low mound-shaped shrub for a sunny spot with well-drained soil. In mild areas, the silver foliage remains all winter.*

Right: Pernettya mucronata *'Mulberry Wine'. This unusual evergreen for acid soil has white bell flowers in early summer. Birds dislike the berries, so they persist on the plant in winter.*

Below: *Hebes, heathers, dwarf rhododendrons and small conifers create an undulating 'mini-landscape' that looks good all year round, but still has room for seasonal interest such as spring bulbs.*

Using compact shrubs

Compact shrubs are not the poor relatives of 'normal' varieties - on the contrary, they include some very choice and exclusive plants. Some of the better-known compact shrubs, such as *Hebe, Cistus* and miniature roses, can be found in most good garden centers, but for more unusual kinds, such as the pea-flowered *Indigofera* and *Baptisia*, look in specialist small nurseries. Alpine plant nurseries often stock a good range of interesting dwarf shrubs, too. Try dwarf willows (*Salix boydii* and *lanata*), and *Helichrysum selago*, which has whipcordlike stems. Most compact shrubs need reasonably good growing conditions - well-drained but moisture-retentive soil - to thrive. This apparent contradiction simply means that the soil should contain plenty of organic matter to hold moisture, but surplus water must be able to drain away, not make the ground boggy. To make the most of compact shrubs, team them with plants on the same scale so that they do not look out of proportion. Small herbaceous plants and carpet-forming rock plants are much more suitable than massive delphiniums and lupins in a mixed border. Alternatively, use a bed of compact shrubs to provide fine detail between trees or normal-sized shrubs. And a formal bed full of miniature roses makes a good low-maintenance alternative to bedding plants; the plants will flower all summer but need not be replaced each season. Train a few as short standards, for extra interest.

Compact shrubs

Berberis *'Corallina Compacta'*, *'Bagatelle'* and thunbergii atropurpurea *'Nana'*
Caryopteris clandonensis *(blue spiraea)*
Ceanothus thyrsiflorus *'Repens'*
Ceratostigma willmottianum *(hardy plumbago)*
Cistus
Convolvulus cneorum
Daphne mezereum
Genista lydia *(a dwarf broom)*
Hardy fuchsia
Hebe
Helianthemum
Indigofera heterantha *(indigo bush)*
Myrtus communis *'Tarentina'* *(myrtle)*
Pernettya mucronata
Phygelius aequalis *(cape figwort)*
Rosemary
Weigela florida *'Variegata'* and *'Foliis Purpureis'*

Left: Dwarf rhododendrons are naturally compact and full of flower in late spring. They need acid soil, but are suitable for growing in pots of ericaceous compost if the garden soil is not right for them.

Right: A selection of reliable and colorful shrubs suitable for the small garden. Be sure to follow the planting advice on the label when you buy them; for example, both the Pieris and the Rhododendron need acid soil.

Left: The hardy plumbago, (Ceratostigma willmottianum), grows into a compact, rounded shape, about 36in(90cm) in height and width. The blue flowers appear in late summer.

Right: The Cape figwort (Phygelius aequalis) from South Africa is smothered in exotic flowers in late summer and early fall. The stems are cut to the ground by frost each winter. This is the variety 'African Queen'.

Skimmia laureola *has greeny-yellow flowers in spring.*

Teucrium fruticans *grows to 48in(120cm) and flowers from early summer until fall.*

Pieris *'Little Heath' has variegated foliage with pink tips in spring.*

Rhododendron *'Blue Tit', a dwarf variety, reaches 30x30in(75x75cm).*

Santolina chamaecyparissius *18x18in(45x45cm). Evergreen with yellow flowers in summer.*

Summer-flowering bulbs

Summer-flowering bulbs such as gladioli and dahlias, and less well-known kinds, including acidanthera, galtonia, tigridia and eucomis, are useful for adding seasonal highlights to the small garden. Plant them between spring-flowering shrubs to extend the season of an existing border or blend them with half-hardy perennials or bedding plants to add dramatic shapes to a vibrant summery color scheme. Gladiolus and dahlias are good for cutting - grow a few plants in the vegetable garden to avoid spoiling your border and keep a few 'spares' handy to tuck into any odd gaps that appear in a border, too. Most summer-flowering bulbs are frost tender and do not survive outside during the winter. For this reason, plant them in late spring shortly before the last frost (being several inches underground, the soil insulates them to some extent). They quickly produce spear-shaped leaves, and flower in mid- to late summer. The foliage of some bulbs dies down quite quickly after flowering. In temperate climates, harvest the bulbs before they are killed by sharp frosts. Gladioli, however, often still have quite green foliage when it is time to lift them; cut this off about 4in(10cm) above the corms. Dahlias are the last to be lifted, as they are late flowering. Wait until the first frosts have blackened their foliage, then cut off the old stems about 3in(7.5cm) above the tubers and turn them upside down so that the remaining sap can drain out. Allow all summer bulbs to dry off properly, then dust them with green sulfur fungicide powder to discourage rotting, before storing them in not-quite-dry peat or coir in a frost-free place for the winter.

1 Choose a suitable container. If the tub is designed for both indoor and outdoor use, it may be necessary to drill holes in the base for drainage. Avoid cracking the container.

2 Half-fill the container with potting mixture; a soil-based mix is preferable. These tigridia bulbs will provide a succession of shortlived colorful blooms during the summer.

3 Space the bulbs out evenly and press in. The dried roots will help you to plant them the right way up. Keep one type of bulb per container; a mixture will flower at different times.

4 Fill the container to the rim with more of the same potting mixture. Allow the soil to settle under its own weight, rather than firming it down.

Here, 15 bulbs fit within a pot 12in(30cm) square.

Left: *Summer-flowering bulbs in pots put on a fine display of blooms in a sunny spot. These are the pale spikes of* Eucomis bicolor *(pineapple flower) and the pink-striped flowers of* Hippeastrum reticulatum *'Striatifolium'.*

Above: *Choose miniature gladioli for the small garden; huge, hybrid kinds tend to be overpowering. These are* Gladiolus nanus *'Prince Claus'.*

Left: Galtonia candicans *(summer hyacinth) has striking spikes of almost fluorescent white flowers. Show them off against a cool green background.*

5 Water in. Stand the container in a sheltered, sunny spot, and water it whenever the soil starts to feel dry. Apply a liquid feed once a week after the shoots are 6in(15cm) high.

Above: Tigridia pavonia *'Rubra'. You can sometimes buy individual colors of bulbs.*

Left: *The tigridia foliage fills the container just before the flower spikes appear.*

Tigridia

Tigridia *(peacock flowers) are bulbous plants that come originally from Mexico. The plants grow to 12in(30cm) tall and have spectacular flowers with three large, triangular-shaped petals in brilliant colors, often heavily spotted, during mid- to late summer. The bulbs are not hardy and cannot be left outdoors during the winter. Plant them outdoors in early summer or in pots several weeks earlier, and keep them in a frost-free place until it is safe to move them outdoors. The bulbs in pots will flower several weeks earlier than those planted in the ground.*

Left: Ground cover roses such as 'Nozomi', pictured here, naturally have a sprawling habit. When grafted onto an upright stem, they make a very attractive small weeping rose tree with bloom-laden branches 36in(90cm) long.

Compact roses

Roses are by far the most popular flowering shrubs, judging from nursery sales statistics. But fashions in roses have changed over the years, and nowadays compact varieties are gaining in popularity. These range from the smallest miniature roses, which grow 12-18in(30-45cm) high, through patio roses, which are like very compact hybrid teas and floribundas perhaps 24-30in(60-75cm) tall, to ground cover roses, which are almost prostrate but may be fairly wide spreading. (They are best planted through a plastic mulch disguised with a layer of bark chippings or soil, as it is difficult - not to say painful - weeding between their thorny interlocking stems). Another development is the reappearance of traditional standard and half-standard roses, with a ball-like head on a tall bare stem. These were once favorites in formal rose gardens, and are great for adding height to a border. Specially stunning are the 'weeping' rose trees, produced when ground cover roses, such as 'Nozomi', are grafted onto a standard stem - the result looks like a waterfall of flowers, perfect for a small tree in a really tiny garden, though like other compact roses, they can be grown in containers, too. However, compact varieties of both normal modern roses and the newly popular old-fashioned roses can be found between the pages of specialist rose nursery catalogs. Like their more ebullient cousins, compact roses thrive best in a sunny spot on heavyish soil - clay loam is their favorite - that is neither waterlogged in winter nor too dry during the summer.

1 Choose a pot in proportion to the size of the rose, and enough soil-based potting mixture. Place a little potting mixture over the bottom of the pot.

2 Tip the rose out of its pot without breaking up the ball of roots. Sit it in the center of the new pot, so that the top of the rootball ends up about 0.5in(1.25cm) below the rim.

3 Holding the plant upright, fill the gap between the root-ball and the sides of the pot with potting mixture. Firm down gently. Make sure there is 0.5in(1.25cm) clear below the rim of the pot for watering.

Patio rose 'Teeny Weeny'. These small plants bring seasonal color to an all-year-round display of evergreens.

4 Water the rose well to settle the new soil around the roots. The plant will need plenty of water in warm weather - the saucer allows water to be soaked up, but tip away any surplus in wet weather.

Right: *Miniature roses are sometimes mistaken for indoor plants, but they are meant for outdoors in beds or tubs. As they are slightly less hardy than normal full-sized varieties, prune them in spring to remove any tips of shoots damaged by frost. This is 'Anna Ford'.*

Miniature/ patio rose 'Gentle Touch'

5 For best effect, group several potted roses together with pots of foliage plants or annuals.

1 *Choose a large watertight container at least 12in(30cm) in diameter and the same depth. Cover the base with 1in(2.5cm) of washed gravel.*

2 *Place three bricks in the bottom, two on end and the middle one flat, to make a 'compartment' that will hold the pump securely in place.*

Water feature in a tub

Water is a great 'plus' in a small garden. The sight, sounds and reflections all add an extra dimension to the surroundings, besides being very therapeutic. But it is not always practical to have a conventional pond. A pond may not fit into the layout or style of the garden; there may not be enough room, or there may be young children for whom standing water would consititute a safety hazard. In any of these cases, it is still possible to include water features, as long as they are of the fountain type. Various ready-made fountain features are available from water garden specialists. These do not need a water supply laid on, as they work by recycling a reservoir of water via a small submersible pump. You can find formal wall-mounted fountains - such as the familiar lion's mask - that spill into a shallow dish. There are millstone features, where water gushes up through the center of a grindstone and runs away between cobbles. Various companies make decorative bowls incorporating small fountains or water trickling over rocks; these are often suitable for indoor or outdoor use (check with the maker). However, you can make the same sort of thing quite easily at home, using very simple 'ingredients'. If you are worried about leaving any container of water where children or animals have access, simply fill it with large pebbles. This effectively prevents anyone from falling in, yet still allows it to be full of water so that you can run a fountain. It also looks good and produces quite musical sounds when a fountain cascades over the top. Remember to top the water level up regularly, as it will gradually drop due to evaporation, especially in warm or windy weather.

Potting a marginal plant

1 *Marginal plants are sold in spring at garden centers. Repot them into perforated plastic baskets. Put a handful of gravel in the base of the basket to weight it down.*

3 Use the smallest available submersible pump and sit it in place between the bricks. Pull out the extension tube, through which the water will be pumped, to its maximum height.

4 An inner container to hold the plants, like this one made from a laundry basket, allows the fountain up-pipe through the middle. It is easy to lift out, but is not essential.

5 Fill the container with gravel to within a pot's depth of the rim. If you did not use the inner container, simply fill the potted pond with pebbles or gravel, covering the pump to the same depth.

2 Place some aquatic potting mix or ordinary garden soil (taken from a spot where no fertilizer has been used) into the bottom of the basket, covering the gravel.

3 Tip the plant out of its original pot and sit it in the center of the basket. Use more of the fertilizer-free potting mix to fill the gap between the rootball and the sides of the container.

4 Use gravel to fill the top 1in(2.5cm)of the basket, right up to the rim. This helps to hold the pot down in the water and also prevents the soil from floating out when the pot is placed on the marginal shelf in the pond.

1 *Make a selection of varied marginal plants, pot them into perforated plastic pond baskets and stand them round the edge of the potted pond.*

2 *Include a few sprawling kinds that will creep out over the edge of the container, and some with colored foliage for extra impact. Many garden centers stock a good range.*

Adding the plants

Choosing plants for small water features needs care; many water plants for conventional ponds grow quickly and get far too big. Miniature water lilies, which grow happily in 12in (30cm) of water, and floating aquatics, such as fairy moss (*Azolla*), water hyacinth and water lettuce, are suitable for growing in a half-barrel or similar-sized container. However, if you want to include a fountain feature, choose marginal plants. These can grow in anything from permanently boggy soil to shallow water, and are ideal for growing in pebbles in a container of water, plunged in pots to their rims. They will also enjoy the cooling effect of splashes from a nearby fountain. (Water lilies, surprisingly, do not grow well when their leaves are being regularly wetted in this way). Choose plants with a naturally striking appearance, with strong shapes and, where possible, colored or variegated foliage, as the flowering season for many pond plants is quite short. By restricting them in pots, their growth will be less vigorous than usual, but they are likely to have overfilled the available space after a year's growth, so divide and repot them every spring. Simply tip them out of their pots, divide, and repot only one of the best pieces from around the edge of the old plant back into the same pot, as described on page 76-77.

3 *Hide the edge of the inner container with pebbles. Put a layer of them over the surface of the gravel between the plants to disguise the plastic edge of the pond and bury the rims of the plant pots.*

4 *Place the nozzle over the pipe from the submerged pump. The type of nozzle you choose determines the style of the fountain produced. Some makers provide several alternatives.*

5 Fill the pond carefully. The water should come up almost to the rim of the container, otherwise the pump will be starved of water and cannot work properly.

Right: A cross section of the potted pond. Similar ponds are available ready-made, but it is cheaper, and more satisfying, to create your own using everyday items.

Marginal plants in perforated plastic pots.

The upturned lid of a plastic laundry basket acts as a tray to carry the water plants.

Bricks support the 'plant tray' and provide a firm foundation for the pump.

Iris pseudacorus 'Variegata'

Geum rivalis

Marsh marigold (Caltha palustris)

Ranunculus repens 'Pleniflorus'

Lobelia cardinalis 'Queen Victoria'

6 Switch on the pump. This nozzle creates a low, formal, bell-shaped cascade that produces a restful gurgling sound, yet spills back accurately into the pond without wetting the surrounding area.

Above: This nozzle produces an informal spray. In windy conditions the water is likely to fall outside the pond, with the result that a small pond can run dry, as it only recirculates its own water. Top up a potted pond at regular intervals.

79

Small water features

Today's water features are informal and fun for all the family. Even a shallow pond attracts wildlife, especially if it is surrounded with a fringe of plants and given gently shelving edges. Natural ponds surrounded with waterside wild flowers are popular, but as these plants can be invasive, weed out unwanted seedlings and divide overgrown clumps in early spring. Alternatively, plant moisture-loving border plants, such as hostas and astilbes, or mound up soil behind a pond to create a rock garden. You could use a compact submersible pump to create a small stream by recycling water from the pond, which tumbles over the rocks or down a preformed chute back into the pond. However, small ponds do need a certain amount of maintenance. During the growing season, pull out excess oxygenating plants, such as Canadian pondweed, (needed to provide oxygen if you have fish). Control blanketweed not with chemicals, but by growing plenty of plants that shade the surface of the water, such as water lilies, fairy moss *(Azolla)* or water lettuce. Do not grow deciduous trees or shrubs too close to the pond, as fallen leaves will rot in the water. Put a net over the surface in the fall to catch leaves, then leave it in place over winter to stop herons stealing your fish.

Right: *Where small children have access to the garden, it is safest to keep to fountain features, such as this gushing grindstone, where there is no standing water to pose a problem.*

Left: A small water feature, packed with detail in the shape of ornaments and surrounding plants, can be every bit as engrossing as a full-sized pond.

Above: A small pond should look restful; as an alternative to colorful flowering marginal plants, especially in a slightly shady spot, try a blend of greens, such as ferns and bamboos.

Left: If you keep fish in a pond, it is vital to include some oxygenating plants for them, plus plenty of marginals and water lilies to provide shade and hiding places.

Right: Another pond alternative is a shallow trough for birds and wildlife to drink from, set amid natural surroundings of grasses and flowers.

Wildlife gardening on a small scale

Above: A small tortoiseshell butterfly feeds on the star-shaped flowers of a ice plant (Sedum spectabile).

Even small gardens can make useful habitats for the prettier wildflowers, which can be grown on their own, or amongst cultivated plants. Honesty, wild strawberry and sweet violets are useful in shade; ladies smock *(Cardamine pratensis)* and wild primroses enjoy wet heavy soil, while ox-eye daisies and maiden pinks are ideal for a dry sunny spot. Heartsease and cowslips thrive in open conditions, though like most wildflowers they prefer low fertilizer levels. Avoid invasive plants, such as celandine or bluebells, which can easily become a nuisance in a small garden. Flowers that attract beneficial insects such as bees (needed to pollinate fruit trees) and hoverflies (which feed on greenfly), and pretty kinds like butterflies are specially desirable. Many cultivated plants are valuable sources of nectar for adult insects, while caterpillars need suitable wildflowers to feed on. Though not very ornamental, a patch of nettles makes a particularly good nursery for caterpillars, as several species will feed on it. The best way to be sure of attracting plenty of different insects is to avoid using any chemical pesticides in the garden, and to grow as many different kinds of flowers as possible - wildflowers, old-fashioned hardy annuals, herbaceous plants and traditional cottage garden flowers (those with single flowers) are the most attractive to a wide range of insects.

1 Group wildflowers together that need similar conditions; cowslips and snakeshead fritillary like moist soil and partial shade.

2 When planting wildflowers in existing grass, cut out circles of turf slightly larger than the diameter of the pots the plants are growing in when you buy them.

3 Scoop out more soil to make the planting holes slightly deeper than the depth of the pots, and loosen the soil at the base of each hole to help the new roots to grow out easily.

Flowers for butterflies and bees

Buckwheat
Buddleia davidii
Calendula marigolds
Comfrey
Heathers
Lavender
Marjoram
Michaelmas daisy
Pulmonaria (*lungwort*)
Sedum spectabile

4 *Gently knock each plant out of its pot and place it carefully into the planting hole, firming the rootball lightly down with your fingertips to help the plant become established.*

5 *For the best effect, make groups of three or five plants, and position them to look as natural as possible - do not plant them in straight rows.*

6 *Water the new plants in well. Water them again whenever the soil is dry until they are established. Do not remove dead heads after flowering; allow the plants to set seed.*

Below: *The orange flowers of calendula marigolds are strongly scented and will attract a wide variety of butterflies and bees to the garden.*

Front gardens filled with flowers

If your front garden is really tiny and you like plenty of color, why not fill it with flowers, leaving just a path or 'stepping stones' to work from? The secret of success is good-quality, fertile, weed-free soil. Eradicate perennial weeds, such as bindweed, with a systemic weedkiller or smother them under black plastic. Improve the ground with plenty of well-rotted organic matter. If the soil is heavy clay, fork in coarse grit to aerate it. Clear away any rubble and add new topsoil if neccesary. If the soil is really poor and thin, make raised beds 6-12in(15-30cm) high. Annual bedding plants make a solid floral display, but if the ground is weed-free, try sowing hardy annuals, such as cornflower, godetia and calendula marigolds, directly into the soil. Alternatively, mix together several packets of seed and scatter them for a random cottage garden effect.

Where weeds are a problem, plant established young plants. Do not plant half-hardy annual bedding plants until after the last frost. Use them with half-hardy perennials for a Mediterranean-style display. In the fall, put in spring bulbs, winter pansies, and primroses, wallflowers and forget-me-nots for a spring display.

Right: Pots of colorful seasonal flowers turn bare concrete paths and hollow-topped walls into valuable garden space, and add to the permanant display of plants in the tiny borders. Bright red azalea blooms provide the largest splashes of color.

Right: A raised front garden creates well-drained conditions for spring bulbs and rockery plants. They provide seasonal highlights to a year-round backdrop of dwarf conifers and heathers.

Cheiranthus *'Bowles Mauve'*

Primula
denticulata

Dicentra
formosa

Dicentra
spectabilis *'Alba'*

Ranunculus
asiaticus
hybrid

Narcissus
'Hawera'

Primula vulgaris
'Flore Plena'

Bergenia
'Ballawley'

Doronicum
orientale

Viola
'Prince Henry'

Pansy

Pansy

Cultivated primrose

Tulip
'Orange Nassau'

Cultivated
primrose

Cultivated primrose

Primula rosea
'Grandiflora'

Pansy

85

Looking at low-maintenance front gardens

Small front gardens, overlooked by passers-by and traffic, are used very differently to back gardens. Often little more than a service route to the house and garage, they may have to double as extra car parking space, too. A conventional garden of grass and borders is much less practical here than a hard surface of paving or concrete. However, a utility front garden can still be decorative. Use an attractive surface (perhaps cobbles, reconstituted stone or molded concrete), leave space for small beds and make good use of containers. But the most versatile hard surface is gravel. Gravel can be laid over landscaping fabric to suppress weeds, allowing specimen shrubs or drifts of low, ground-covering plants to be planted through it. Junipers, hypericum, rosemaries, thymes and other drought-tolerant perennials, especially evergreen kinds, are ideal. Alternatively, you can achieve a casual 'cottagey' look by laying the gravel straight over soil and allowing plants in nearby beds to seed themselves randomly. Wallflowers, *Alyssum saxatile, Viola labradorica*, euphorbias, etc. will all 'wander' happily.

Containers are a useful way of adding height to groups of plants, but also look decorative 'outlining' doors and gateways, and there is the added advantage that you can move them around. Where vehicles are to be parked, reinforce the gravel with a deep layer of hardcore underneath, and use tall containers to mark the boundaries of the parking area to avoid accidents to nearby plants. Expect a few weeds to appear through the gravel, but these are easy to pull out or deal with by squirting with a spot weeder.

Left: Permanent features, such as the striking paving and black metal obelisks, which have been chosen to match the garden railings, help to establish the character of this tiny but impressive front garden.

Right: In a really tiny space, grow plants up walls and in containers for a clean but simple effect. However, take care to leave access ways clear, so that they do not get in the way of visitors or essential services.

Left: *Gravel, brick paths, dwarf box hedges and a framework of evergreens keep this garden looking good all year round, yet because of the dense cover of foliage in the beds, there is very little weeding to do.*

Below: *A bold, formal design makes the most of 'hard' features, such as paving and twist-top edging tiles, and keeps beds to a minimum, so this garden looks striking without needing much work to maintain.*

Plants for security

Are you fed up with vandals picking your flowers - or worried about burglars? Then why not let your garden join the fight against crime. First fit a security light with an infrared sensor that detects movement and lights up whenever anyone comes into the garden. Add a secure gate at the side of the house to prevent intruders going round to the back. Next, design the front garden so that the center is open and not obscured by large shrubs, so that you can see it all clearly from the house. Plant a hedge or a wide border of prickly plants along the edge of the garden bordering the street - roses, berberis, chaenomeles or double-flowered gorse all make a good, impenetrable barrier yet look decorative. Alternatively, grow the sort of plants that will quickly recover if odd branches are snapped off, such as ornamental currant (*Ribes*), *Symphoricarpos*, *Senecio* 'Sunshine', *Spiraea*, *Cornus* and heathers. Grow flowers that are deep-rooted and difficult to pull up and, ideally, have unpleasant slimy sap or smell strongly when damaged, as this does have an effect; daffodils, rue, *Hypericum* and lemon balm (*Melissa officinalis*) are good choices.

Although many plants are difficult to pull up once they are well established, if you think plants may be pulled out, secure their rootballs firmly when you plant them, using one or more long wire 'hairpins' before covering them with soil. Cover paths and the drive with gravel, as the scrunching sound provides audible warning of visitors. Avoid putting hanging baskets or troughs at the front of the house unless they are too heavy to be removed.

Mahonia japonica 'Winter Sun' an evergreen with many spiky leaflets.

Ilex aquifolium 'Ferox Argentea' is a variegated hedgehog holly with spikes on the leaf surface and round the edge.

Berberis thunbergii 'Aurea' is a dense, spiny shrub.

The climbing patio rose 'Warm Welcome' ('Chewizz') has protective spines.

Osmanthus heterophyllus 'Goshiki' ('Tricolor') has variegated, sharp, hollylike leaves.

Above: Hypericum calycinum *emits an unpleasant smell when it is damaged - a natural defense against plant thieves or vandals entering the garden.*

Left: Senecio 'Sunshine' *soon replaces damaged growth and makes good all-year-round ground cover under roses - this one is 'Ballerina', a thorny type.*

Below: Rosa rugosa *and its cultivars, such as 'Alba' shown here, make good thorny hedges. The plants produce large, single flowers followed by huge tomato-like hips, much loved by birds.*

Trees for small gardens

Most trees grow too large and too quickly to be anything but a nuisance in a small garden. A large tree casts heavy shade, sheds many leaves that block gutters and clog ponds, and has roots that may damage foundations and drains if an unsuitable species is planted too close to the house. However, no garden is complete without a tree; the trick is to choose one that stays compact and will not cause structural problems, as well as providing interest over a long season. Many of the trees sold as suitable for small gardens - weeping birch, *Amelanchier*, *Prunus* 'Amanogawa' (a narrow upright flowering cherry) and ornamental crab apples - can nevertheless grow too big for a real pocket handkerchief-type of garden. In these cases, it is best to look for trees that have either been specially trained into compact forms, such as cordon apples and pears, or grown on specially dwarfing rootstocks (some ornamental crab apples), or which are genetic dwarfs (patio peaches). Some shrubs can be pruned to form very compact trees; Japanese maples, *Prunus incisa* (Mount Fuji cherry), *Garrya elliptica* and *Arbutus unedo* (strawberry tree) are often sold trained this way, though it is cheaper to start with a small bushy plant and train your own by removing a few of the lower branches every spring. It is also possible to 'cheat' by growing trees in containers. This keeps them small by restricting the roots. In this way you could grow a large collection of trees without problems, but they will need frequent watering and annual repotting. Put them back into the same container with fresh potting mix after pruning the roots slightly.

Kilmarnock willow
(Salix caprea *'Pendula'*)

Acer palmatum
'Dissectum Viridis'

Left: One of the dwarf forms of the Mount Fuji cherry, Prunus incisa 'Kojo-no-mai', forms a dense twiggy shape, covered in starry blossom in spring. It has the added bonus of attractive fall tints later in the year.

Naturally small trees

Betula 'Trost's Dwarf'
(dwarf birch)
Hibiscus syriacus
(hardy hibiscus)
Morus nigra *(mulberry)*
Prunus incisa 'Kojo no mai'
(dwarf form Mount Fuji cherry)
Prunus subhirtella 'Pendula'
Salix lanata
Salix caprea 'Pendula'
(Kilmarnock willow)
Standard roses

Standard roses need a site sheltered from late frosts to avoid dieback, which can kill off the entire head.

Left: Cercis siliquastrum, the Judas tree, produces waxy flowers in early summer that grow, without stems, straight from the trunk and branches. This is a specially striking deeper pink-flowered form.

Above: This 'Sweet Magic' patio rose has been trained as a standard and will attain the height of the stem onto which it was grafted. When grown as a bush it reaches 18in(45cm) high.

Fruit trees for small gardens

Below: The morello cherry is traditionally fan-trained, but it can also be grown as a free-standing tree. The fruit is used for cooking.

If you insist on a traditional, free-standing fruit tree, you will not have room for more than one in a small garden. However, by taking advantage of dwarfing rootstocks and compact training methods, it is possible to fit in a good range of fruit. Apple and pear trees, grown on very dwarfing rootstocks, are commonly sold as cordons, which look like trunks with fruit produced from small clusters of short twigs along their length. These can be planted as 'fruiting screens', about 24in(60cm) apart, along a post and wire support framework. If you prefer a traditional tree shape, go for a 'family' tree, on which each branch is a different variety but they all grow on one trunk. The varieties chosen all cross-pollinate each other, so you are sure of a crop, but family trees are either apple or pear, not both. On a wall, fan-trained fruits, such as figs, apricots, peaches or nectarines, look decorative and do specially well. Cherries and plums are not readily available on very dwarfing rootstocks, and the trees grow too big for very small gardens. But why not try unusual fruits instead? Ornamental crab apples are available on dwarfing rootstocks, and varieties like 'John Downie' make great jelly. Mulberries grow slowly and make umbrella-shaped small trees with gnarled trunks; named varieties fruit within a few years of planting. Vines produce good crops of grapes trained along walls and fences or over pergolas, and can also be trained as standard plants for growing in pots. Lemons and kumquats are the hardiest of the citrus plants, and though they do not survive outside except in very mild areas, they make good plants for growing in large pots on a patio in summer.

Above: Espalier-trained apples make productive use of wall space, but make sure they receive plenty of sun. This variety is 'Orleans Reinette'.

Below: Kumquats are citrus fruits that look like small oval oranges. The trees are not hardy, so grow them in pots kept at above 45°F(7°C) in winter and stand them out on a sunny patio in summer.

Fan-trained apple 'Red Devil'

Bush apple 'Gala'

Ballerina apple tree

Left: *Fruit trees grafted onto moderately dwarfing rootstocks can remain in large pots for many years, provided they are kept well fed and watered during the growing season.*

Above: *A grapevine is a productive way of covering trellis or pergola poles in a sheltered sunny spot outdoors. Be sure to choose an outdoor variety.*

'Fiesta'

'Discovery'

'Sunset'

Left: *If you have room for only one fruit tree, choose a family tree. This tree has several varieties of apple on one trunk, each chosen to cross-pollinate the next so that you can be sure of a good crop.*

Right: *Choose a healthy young vine and plant it 18in(45cm) away from the base of a wall. Train the main stem up onto its supports via a cane.*

93

Fruit bushes for small gardens

Few small gardens have space for fruit bushes, although a row of good varieties, well cared for, can be surprisingly productive. Grow them as a hedge, screening off the vegetable garden or compost heap, or grow cane fruit, such as loganberries on a fence. However, if there is no other way, try substituting a few fruit bushes for regular shrubs in an ornamental border. Red and white currant, red gooseberry and josta berry (a hybrid between blackcurrant and gooseberry) all have attractive blossom followed by pretty fruit that puts many 'ornamental' shrubs to shame. On a wall, kiwi fruit are productive and pretty - choose a dual-sex variety such as 'Hayward' so that you only need one plant. Make use of shady areas under shrubs to grow a luscious crop of alpine or wild strawberries. For more open situations, such as the front of a border, normal strawberry varieties are now available with pink flowers instead of white, which look decorative and also give good crops of fruit. On acid soil, ericaceous fruit can be added to a border of rhododendrons, etc. - blueberries and cranberries are both most attractive plants. When growing fruit in a border with flowers, do not expect such heavy crops as when the same plants are grown in a separate fruit garden, because competition from surrounding plants will reduce yields. Feed, mulch and water fruit bushes more often than usual to compensate for this, and give them reasonably generous spacing. And remember to protect ripening fruit from the birds by draping net curtains or crop protection netting over individual bushes when necessary.

Above: Redcurrants are as attractive as many flowering shrubs, but have the added advantage of a productive edible crop.

Left: Redcurrants are traditionally grown on a short 'leg' like gooseberries. This makes them easy to weed and mulch beneath. Prune them in the same way as gooseberries, too.

Right: Blueberries, such as 'Ivanhoe' shown here, need acid soil to grow in. If the garden soil is not suitable, grow them in containers of ericaceous potting mixture.

Left: *Whitecurrants have fruit like strings of pearls dangling from the branches. They are ornamental enough to include in a shrub border where space is short.*

Right: *Worcesterberry is a hybrid that produces a heavy crop of dark red fruit half way between currants and gooseberries in appearance. The plants make large bushes.*

Fill the gaps between the rootballs with more potting mixture.

This is 'Serenata', which produces a good crop of fruit.

Below: *Strawberries will grow in beds, in rows round the edge of a fruit plot or in containers. Most, such as this 'Elsanta', fruit in early to midsummer.*

Right: *A planter such as this will take at least six strawberry plants. For early fruit, move the container to a cool greenhouse in midwinter.*

Planting strawberries in a growing bag

Growing bags allow you to garden on balconies and paving where there is no soil. They are cheaper than containers filled with potting mixture, as the packaging forms its own 'free' disposable container. Laid end to end, they can create what is effectively a continuous bed along a wall or on a patio and are the perfect way to grow shortlived fruit crops, such as strawberries. To grow strawberries, plant ten young, pot-grown plantlets per bag in spring. The nutrients in the potting mix provide all they need until flowering time, when you should start weekly liquid feeding with a half-strength, high-potash (tomato) feed. Continue feeding after picking the fruit until the end of the growing season. The following year, start feeding as soon as the plants make new growth in spring, as before. This time, after fruiting, discard both the old plants and bag, which you can tip on the garden to improve the soil, and start afresh the following spring. If there is space in a greenhouse or conservatory in early spring, you can 'force' growing bags of strawberries to give early fruit. Wait until a few weeks after midwinter, by which time the plants will have experienced a cold spell, then move them under cover. Hand-pollinate the flowers with a soft brush, as few bees will get in. The higher the temperature, the earlier the plants will crop, but even in an unheated greenhouse, fruit will ripen several weeks earlier than outside.

Above: Alpine strawberries have much smaller fruit then normal kinds, but a distinctive wild strawberry taste. They grow well in slight shade.

1 To conceal the rather 'loud' plastic packaging of the growing bag, it has been placed inside a special growing bag container. Made of tinted plastic, the effect is surprisingly natural.

2 As this growing bag is standing in a container, you can cut open the entire top instead of cutting as directed by the manufacturer. This gives a large open area for planting.

3 Knock ten plants out of their pots
without breaking up the rootballs,
and make a planting hole with a trowel.

4 Plant two rows of five, keeping
each row close to the very edge
of the growing bag to avoid over-
crowding. Both rows can be of the
same variety or plant one row of an
early and one row of a maincrop.

5 After planting, water lightly in.
Avoid overwatering as there are no
drainage holes. When flowers appear,
start feeding weekly with tomato feed.

Vegetables in the small garden

Where space is short, it is best to concentrate on producing small quantities of many different crops, particularly slightly more 'special' ones. As well as providing an interesting range of tastes for the table, they also look good enough to grow in the flower garden if you do not have room for a separate vegetable garden. Give vegetables adequate spacing when growing them with flowers, feed and water them regularly and protect them from slugs and other pests. Support peas by growing them up through 'cage' supports sold for herbaceous flowers or with twiggy sticks. Beans and outdoor cucumbers grow well on trellis or up tripods of canes. For top productivity from a small space, go for mangetout or snap peas - eaten shell and all - New Zealand spinach and runner beans (which both crop heavily all summer). But for sheer flavor, choose climbing French beans. Pretty crops, good for growing with flowers, include golden courgettes, purple-podded beans, runner beans, red-leaved beetroot and red-stemmed Swiss chard. Fashionable 'baby' vegetables such as tiny leeks, turnips, beetroot, early carrots and kohl rabi, are best grown on a well-prepared deep bed by sowing as usual and leaving plants much closer together when thinning out (about two-thirds the normal recommended spacing. Hurry the crops along with plenty of water and a regular, weak liquid feed, and pick them while still tiny. To prepare a deep bed, dig the soil very deeply and add plenty of well-rotted organic matter. Thereafter, do not walk on the soil to avoid compacting it and preventing the roots from penetrating freely. Deep beds are usually only 36-48in(90-120cm) wide, so that you can work on them from either side. Once prepared, the bed need not be dug again. At the end of each growing season, top up the beds with more organic matter, either roughly forked in or left on the surface for worms to draw down into the soil.

Above: Edible crops and ornamental plants look decorative. Try outdoor cucumbers with climbing nasturtiums and lettuce, beetroot and herbs, as here.

Right: Miniature bush tomatoes, such as 'Tumbler', produce heavy crops of smallish but delicious fruit. Feed the plants regularly for best results.

Left: *In a small space, crops that taste best eaten fresh from the garden, such as peas and lettuce, also make the best use of the available room. Sow both often for successional cropping.*

Below: *Use valuable wall space for climbing crops, such as runner beans, with courgettes below. Mixing the two makes a more decorative effect without seriously affecting yields.*

Growing lettuce

A space about 6ft square (about 4m²) is all you need to grow salads. Good fertile soil with plenty of organic matter and a sunny spot are essential. To keep a continuous supply throughout the summer, sow a few seeds of lettuce every two or three weeks.

Slugs and snails are fond of young salad leaves, so take anti-mollusk measures. Make sure that the salads do not shade each other, and apply liquid feeds regularly to keep them growing well.

Below: *'Carnival' and 'Red salad bowl' lettuce with chicory.*

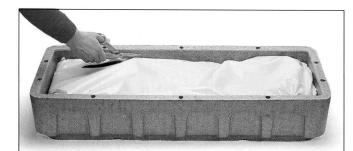

1 *You can hide highly colored growing bags in a suitably sized, free-standing trough. Start cutting into the plastic with a pair of scissors.*

2 *In a trough, the sides of the bag are supported, so you can cut out the top of the bag completely, which gives you a much larger planting area.*

3 *Turn back the edges of the plastic to form a raised 'lip', which helps prevent water running off - a common problem when watering growing bags.*

Space-saving vegetables

Small-scale gardeners regularly complain that they have no room to grow vegetables, but why not grow a few of your favorite edible crops in containers? Large tubs, troughs, and growing bags are all useful ways of converting 'wasted' space into productive cropping area. All you need is a narrow strip along a path, in a corner of a patio or even on a balcony, windowbox or flat roof (if it is sufficiently strong and has easy access). Do not bother with crops that take up a great deal of space or are cheap to buy in the shops; go for those that taste best picked garden-fresh. French beans, outdoor cucumbers, tomatoes, baby new potatoes, peppers, frilly red lettuce and golden courgettes, herbs and salad leaves, such as rocket and purslane, are all ideal choices. Growing bags and containers of potting mixture can be used several times over, as long as you plant completely different crops each time. Plant cucumbers, tomatoes or peppers first, as these are most sensitive to root problems, and follow with spinach, courgettes, potatoes and lettuce. Keep crops regularly fed from planting onwards, especially when reusing old potting mixture. Feed heavy-fruiting crops, such as tomatoes and peppers, with liquid tomato feed, and leafy crops including lettuce, beans and cucumbers, with general-purpose liquid feed. Stand containers of vegetables in a sheltered sunny spot, and check them daily to see if they need watering. Growing bags are particularly prone to drying out quickly when crops are tall and putting on rapid growth.

4 *Knock the plants out of their pots and plant without disturbing the rootballs. These are bush courgette plants; plant two per growing bag.*

Beans in a growing bag

Dwarf and climbing beans do well in growing bags. Water in and start feeding with general-purpose liquid feed weekly after three weeks. Dwarf beans need no support, but place climbers alongside a wall with trellis or wire netting for them to grow up, or make a framework of canes to stand over the bag.

Plant two rows of six plants down each side of the bag.

Above: 'Sugar snap' peas have an excellent taste and do well in growing bags. They need a sheltered, sunny site. Put plants out in late spring or sow seeds into the bags then.

Peppers in a growing bag

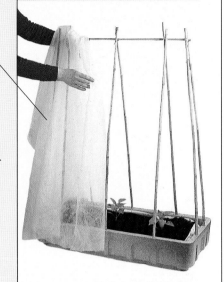

The fleece allows light to penetrate, but protects plants.

Right: Plant three pepper plants per growing bag. The plants need plenty of warmth and shelter, so make a framework of canes and fix crop protection fleece over like a 'tent' until the weather warms up.

Below: Plant three tomato plants per bag. Bush varieties are best outdoors, but support them on canes. These slip into holes in the walls of this trough, which is made to take growing bags.

5 After planting and gently firming in, water the soil well so that it is evenly moist. Then water sparingly until plants are growing faster, when they will need more frequent watering.

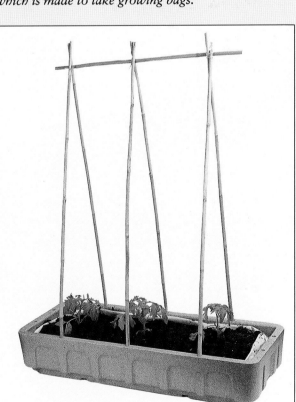

101

Growing potatoes in a tub

Sit each potato with the end containing the 'eyes' uppermost.

You can grow all kinds of potatoes in containers, but it is more practical to grow early (new) potatoes or 'specialist' varieties that are difficult to find in the shops. Early varieties can be produced even earlier than usual by planting the tubers six weeks earlier than recommended and keeping the container in a frost-free greenhouse or sunroom until after the last frost. Then move the container outdoors. Expect to gather the crop in early midsummer, leaving the container free to be planted up with flowers or other edibles, such as herbs. It is also possible to enjoy 'new' potatoes later in the season by storing a few seed potatoes of an early variety in a cool, shady spot and planting them after gathering the first crop of earlies. These will be ready to harvest from the fall onwards. However, remember to bring the container back into a frost-free growing environment before the first frosts, as potatoes are not hardy. Specialist gourmet potatoes grown for their fine flavor include both early and maincrop varieties. 'Belle de Fountenay', 'Pink Fir Apple' and 'Linzer Delikatess' are especially tasty. Early potatoes are ready to pick when the first flowers appear on the plants. There is no need to pull up the whole plant; just feel round for the largest potatoes and leave the others to grow for a bit longer. Leave maincrop potatoes until the foliage starts to yellow naturally before pulling them up, but again you can take a few potatoes before this stage. Keep potatoes well fed and watered during the growing period and buy new seed potatoes the following year.

1 *Buy seed potatoes in early spring and sit them on end to sprout. Keep them at cool to normal room temperature in daylight.*

2 *Shovel 3in(7.5cm) of potting mixture into the bottom of a large container. You could reuse old growing bag soil, as long as it has not been used for growing potatoes before.*

3 *When the sprouts on the seed potatoes are 0.5-1in(1.25-2.5cm) long, lay them on the soil in the tub, about 10in(25cm) apart, with the sprouts facing upwards. This tub is big enough to take three.*

Choose healthy tubers with no cuts and bruises, rotten bits or mold on the surface. Damaged tubers are more likely to rot than grow.

4 For maximum productivity, fit in a second 'tier' of potatoes. Shovel another 2in(5cm) of potting mixture into the tub, just deep enough to bury the first lot of potatoes.

5 Place another three potatoes, spaced as before, into the gaps between the potatoes in the previous layer. This way, the tub will be virtually full of potatoes.

6 Fill the tub with soil to within 1in(2.5cm) of the rim to allow for watering. Stand the tub in a sunny sheltered spot outside. Protect from frost.

Left: *Early potato varieties are ready when flowers appear. Do not pull up main crop potatoes until the leaves start yellowing in late midsummer.*

7 Thoroughly moisten the soil, but do not overwater - the tubers take a few weeks to root. When the shoots appear, feed and water regularly.

8 When the plants are growing strongly, keep them regularly watered and feed every 10 days with any good, general-purpose liquid feed.

Curry plant

Rosemary

Purple sage

Parsley

Thyme
'Silver Posie'

Tricolor sage

Chives

Dill

Growing herbs in the small garden

Herbs are always useful, and decorative enough to grow all around the garden - in tubs and windowboxes, between paving stones, in historic-look herb gardens, and in beds with other flowers. The key to growing herbs successfully is soil and site - they like warm, well-drained sunny spots and not too much fertilizer. The basic culinary collection includes herbs such as chives, parsley, rosemary, mint and thyme, to which you could add choicer annuals, including chervil, knotted marjoram, basil and dill. Perennial herbs, such as chives, rosemary and sages - ornamental kinds like purple sage are good for cooking, too - are easily fitted into a sunny border; chives make a nice edging for a path. Mint is rather invasive, best grown in a large pot sunk to its rim in a border to contain it. The less well-known eau-de-cologne mint is specially worth growing; it has a true 'perfume' scent and delicious flavor when cooked with peas or new potatoes. Parsley runs to seed in its second year, so is best treated as an annual. Sow a row along the edge of a path in spring or sprinkle it thinly in pots and thin out, as seedlings do not transplant well. You can pick the same plants regularly all summer. Annuals, such as chervil, basil and dill, are very shortlived and not frost hardy, so sow them in pots on a warm windowsill and transplant after the last frost - sow new batches every six weeks for continuity. If space permits, include less common herbs, too, for occasional use: coriander leaves (for Indian cookery or in salads), french sorrel (boil the leaves like spinach or use it in omelettes), and bay (*Laurus nobilis*), an evergreen shrub that looks superb trained into a pyramid and grown in a tub by the doorstep.

Left: *Thyme is useful in cookery and its flowers attract bees and butterflies. It will grow in a container or hanging basket and creeping varieties flourish when planted between paving stones.*

Right: Herbs combine well in a raised bed growing with an assortment of vegetables. Here, parsley, oregano and purple sage are planted alongside french beans and calabrese.

Mimulus plants provide colorful blooms throughout the growing season.

Above: A collection of mints growing in three terracotta pots, one inside the other. This not only makes an interesting and space saving display, but also allows you to experiment with the many types and scents available and show off their range of color, shape and textures.

Right: Herbs are good plants for hanging baskets as they are naturally quite drought tolerant. This mixture includes parsley, golden marjoram, oregano and lemon variegated thyme, which are colorful and sweetly scented.

Parsley

Golden marjoram

Oregano

Lemon variegated thyme

Index to Plants

Page numbers in **bold** indicate major text references. Page numbers in *italics* indicate captions and annotations to photographs. Other text entries are shown in normal type.

Credits

The majority of the photographs featured in this book have been taken by Neil Sutherland and are © Colour Library Books. The publishers wish to thank the following photographers for providing additional photographs, credited here by page number and position on the page, i.e. (B)Bottom, (T)Top, (C)Center, (BL)Bottom left, etc.

A-Z Botanical Collection Ltd/A. Stenning: 60(TR)
Pat Brindley: 26(BR), 73(TR)
Eric Crichton: 13(TR), 16-17(TC), 17(BC), 18(B), 21(TR), 23(BR), 37(BL), 40-1(T), 43(TR), 57(BR), 59(BL), 60(BL), 64(BR), 69(TC), 71(TL,TR) 73(TC, BR), 75(TR), 81(TR), 86-7(TC), 89(TC,BR), 98(TR), 99(TL,BL), 101(TC), 105(TR)
John Glover: Half-title page, 10, 12(B), 15(R), 16, 20(T), 22(BL), 23(TR), 36(T), 42(BL), 51(BR), 56(B), 58(BR), 60-1(B), 61(TL), 65(TR), 66(TR), 67(TL,TR), 69(TR,BR), 70, 74(TL), 81(L), 82(TL), 83(BL), 84(TR), 94(BR), 104(BL)
Andrew Lawson: 45(CL), 89(TR)
S & O Mathews: 32(BR)
Natural Image/Liz Gibbons: 22-3(TC), 80(TR), 99(BR)
Clive Nichols: Copyright page, 13(TL), 13(BR, Designer Anthony Noel), 14(B, Designer Anthony Noel), 17(R), 18-19(C), 19(TR), 19(BR, Designer Sue Berger), 27(TR,BR), 29(L,TR,BR), 32(BL,TR), 37(BR, Keukenhof Gardens, Holland), 39(TR), 40(BL), 41(BR), 43(BR, Designer Jill Billington), 44(R, Keukenhof Gardens, Holland), 45(R), 46(CR, Designer Anthony Noel), 57(BL), 58(L), 59(TR,BR), 61(R, Keukenhof Gardens, Holland), 62(BR), 80(B), 81(BR), 84(BR, Mrs Voges, Bennebrock, Holland), 86(BL, Designer Jean Bishop), 87(BL), 87(BR, Designer Jean Bishop), 92(TR)
Photos Horticultural: 91(TL), 92(BR), 93(TR), 95(TR,BL), 96(TL), 98(BR)
Daan Smit: 65(TL), 73(TL)
Harry Smith Photographic Collection: 42-43(C), 51(TR), 59(TL), 91(BL)

Acknowledgments

The publishers would like to thank Country Gardens at Chichester for providing plants and photographic facilities during the production of this book; thanks are particularly due to Cherry Burton and Sue Davey for their enthusiastic help and guidance.